Norse Runes and Trolldom

A Guide to Runic Symbols, Rune Divination, Spells, and Traditional Nordic Magic from Sweden, Norway, Denmark, and Finland

© Copyright 2023 - All rights reserved.

The content contained within this book may not be reproduced, duplicated, or transmitted without direct written permission from the author or the publisher.

Under no circumstances will any blame or legal responsibility be held against the publisher, or author, for any damages, reparation, or monetary loss due to the information contained within this book, either directly or indirectly.

Legal Notice:

This book is copyright protected. It is only for personal use. You cannot amend, distribute, sell, use, quote, or paraphrase any part, or the content within this book, without the consent of the author or publisher.

Disclaimer Notice:

Please note the information contained within this document is for educational and entertainment purposes only. All effort has been executed to present accurate, up-to-date, reliable, and complete information. No warranties of any kind are declared or implied. Readers acknowledge that the author is not engaging in the rendering of legal, financial, medical, or professional advice. The content within this book has been derived from various sources. Please consult a licensed professional before attempting any techniques outlined in this book.

By reading this document, the reader agrees that under no circumstances is the author responsible for any losses, direct or indirect, that are incurred as a result of the use of the information contained within this document, including, but not limited to, errors, omissions, or inaccuracies.

Your Free Gift
(only available for a limited time)

Thanks for getting this book! If you want to learn more about various spirituality topics, then join Mari Silva's community and get a free guided meditation MP3 for awakening your third eye. This guided meditation mp3 is designed to open and strengthen ones third eye so you can experience a higher state of consciousness. Simply visit the link below the image to get started.

https://spiritualityspot.com/meditation

Table of Contents

PART 1: ELDER FUTHARK RUNES 1
   INTRODUCTION 2
   CHAPTER 1: INTRODUCTION TO NORSE MYTHOLOGY 4
   CHAPTER 2: THE HISTORY OF THE RUNES 13
   CHAPTER 3: THE RUNIC ALPHABET 22
   CHAPTER 4: THE THREE RUNIC AETTIR 36
   CHAPTER 5: THE MAGIC OF THE RUNES AND STAVES 46
   CHAPTER 6: CREATING AND ACTIVATING YOUR RUNES 56
   CHAPTER 7: SEIÐR: THE ART OF RUNIC DIVINATION 65
   CHAPTER 8: MORE WAYS TO WORK WITH RUNES 74
   CHAPTER 9: NORSE MAGIC IN THE MODERN WORLD 84
   BONUS: LIST OF RUNES AND THEIR SYMBOLISM 93

PART 2: TROLLDOM 104
   INTRODUCTION 105
   CHAPTER 1: INTRODUCING TROLLDOM 106
   CHAPTER 2: THE CYPRIANUS TRADITION 115
   CHAPTER 3: THE POWER OF HERB MAGIC 125
   CHAPTER 4: CAULDRON MAGIC 139
   CHAPTER 5: MAGICAL SWORDS AND DAGGERS 153
   CHAPTER 6: THE USAGE OF CORD MAGIC 162
   CHAPTER 7: UNLOCKING ELF MAGIC 170
   CHAPTER 8: DWARF MAGIC 177
   CHAPTER 9: A GUIDE TO PRACTICING TROLLDOM 185
   BONUS SECTION 195

CONCLUSION 203
HERE'S ANOTHER BOOK BY MARI SILVA THAT YOU MIGHT LIKE 204
YOUR FREE GIFT (ONLY AVAILABLE FOR A LIMITED TIME) 205
REFERENCES 206

Part 1: Elder Futhark Runes

Unlocking Rune Divination, Norse Magic, Spells, and Runic Symbols

Introduction

The runes of Elder Futhark are magical symbols that convey the story of life from its first-ever creation in the Universe to the birth, death, and rebirth of every living being. According to Norse mythology, these forces constantly occur in nature and are also present in all aspects of magic. The Germanic tribes living in Northern Europe centuries ago discovered that runes provided an outlet for natural magic. They also used them as tools to harness natural energy.

This book will help you understand that the Norse runes' magic is not limited by the symbolism of any individual rune. In addition, the meanings of each of the runes are also tied to the meaning of other runes. Elder Futhark runes were initially nothing but a series of sounds, often described as incantations. They were also used to communicate with the spiritual world and nature and express gratitude. All these aspects are valuable tools for a contemporary Norse magic practitioner, regardless of their experience level.

This book will teach you how to use Norse runes in reverse order compared to how they were discovered. Instead of writing down the symbols after familiarizing yourself with their concept as it happened through the centuries, you will first practice writing them as a way to familiarize yourself with their meaning. This is where the user-friendly practical portion of the book will come in handy. This will teach you how to equate the 24 runes of the Elder Futhark with the letters of the Latin alphabet, beginning with F and ending with O.

After practicing their written form, you'll be ready to move on to learn about the three purposes of the runes - communication, divination, and invocations. The second half of this book provides plenty of hands-on techniques to incorporate these intentions into your practice. Not only that, but it'll also enlist all the different meanings associated with each rune.

The number of ways you incorporate Norse runes into magical practices is infinite. This has become more than evident through the recent revival of Asatru, Odinism, and similar Norse magic approaches. Whatever your Norse magic practice entails, expanding your knowledge about the Elder Futhark runes will allow you to access new avenues for divination, spells, and more.

Being the oldest form of the runic alphabet, Elder Futhark represents the gateway to the most elemental and empowering form of magic. So, if you are ready to empower yourself through Norse runes, keep reading. You'll uncover a world that makes using natural magic as easy as breathing. Once you familiarize yourself with all the runic symbolism and learn to create your own, finding ways to enrich your practice will be one of your biggest strengths. After all, divination, spells, spiritual communication, and rituals aren't the only ways to harness energy through runes. You can also incorporate them into your meditation exercises, use them as protection while you sleep, or even wear them as jewelry and other forms of talismans. With all these ways to make you more aware of Norse magic, it's up to you how and when you start implementing them!

Chapter 1: Introduction to Norse Mythology

We can't talk about Elder Futhark runes without mentioning their origin, which was Norse mythology. You may be familiar with Norse mythology since the Marvel characters Thor, Loki, and Odin were all inspired by it. English author Neil Gaiman was also inspired by Norse mythology and wrote a book under the same name. Many of the characters from his novel "American gods" (later turned into a TV show) were based on Norse gods like Loki and Odin. Another English author heavily influenced by Norse mythology is J. R. R. Tolkien, especially in his popular novels Lord of the Rings and The Hobbit. Norse mythology found its way to modern culture along with the Vikings, or Norsemen, portrayed in various movies and TV shows.

The Vikings were a group of people from various countries like Iceland, Norway, Sweden, and Denmark who followed the Norse pagan religion. They were explorers, traders, conquerors, raiders, and settlers. They lived during the appropriately named "Viking Age" from 793 CE to 1066 CE. They traveled to multiple places outside Europe, like ancient Baghdad and North America, which they discovered centuries before Christopher Columbus was even born. They spoke the Old Norse language, a Germanic language, and wrote in runes which we will discuss in detail in the coming chapters.

Various reasons led the Vikings to move from their homeland and conquer the world. However, what they desired more than anything was wealth and power. They left us with many poems, legends, and sagas of their lives during Pre-Christian times. In fact, we know more about the Vikings' religion than any other Germanic religion. However, all Germanic religions shared some similarities with Norse Paganism.

Although Greek and Roman mythologies and their gods are more popular, this doesn't make Norse mythology and its gods and legends any less fascinating. As more and more people discover Norse mythology, its popularity grows, which has left its mark on modern civilization. However, if you think you know everything about Norse mythology after watching a movie or a TV show, we are here to tell you that the real legends are much more fascinating. This chapter will focus on Norse mythology and uncover its many secrets.

What Is Norse Mythology?

We may think we know that Norse mythology was based on what we know about its fearless warriors, the Vikings, or its popular gods, Thor and Loki. However, there is more to it than what is portrayed in modern culture. A big part of Norse mythology was its religion and the various beliefs heavily practiced and followed by European Germanics. The tribes residing in northern and central Europe at the time all practiced the same Norse religion and spoke the same Norse languages. Although various cultures practiced Christianity during the middle ages, the Norsemen remained true to their pagan religion and beliefs.

The Norse religion wasn't different from other religions as it was also based on stories that taught the people moral lessons and helped them understand and learn about the world around them. Norse mythology is a collection of stories and tales of various gods and goddesses. The Vikings found meaning in these stories as they provided them with the wisdom and guidance they needed to live their lives. The Vikings never gave a proper name to their religions like Christianity, Islam, Buddhism, and various other religions. They simply referred to it as "tradition."

If there is one thing all religions share in common, it's the belief in the divine or greater power, and the Norse religion was no different. It had its own methods of worshiping and connecting to the divine. These methods may seem strange and unusual to you at first. However, at their core, they were simply human quests to help people find the joy of being connected to a higher power and live their lives in the presence of the divine. The Vikings saw their world differently. They found everything, whether their culture or nature, to be enchanting and marvelous.

For this reason, they never tried to change things and left them the way they were. This isn't to say that Norse mythology painted the world as a perfect place. On the contrary, their myths acknowledge that life could be unfair and full of misfortunes and sadness. How you deal with these challenges and accomplish good deeds for the greater good can help you live a good life and reach Valhalla.

Valhalla is an old Nordic word that means "the hall of the fallen." It is similar to our modern-day concept of heaven. It is the place or "hall" in the afterlife where Odin (god of the dead and ruler of Valhalla) houses the souls of the dead. It is believed that only brave Viking soldiers who died in battle can go there.

The Vikings didn't just believe in one god. Like the ancient Greeks, Romans, and Egyptians, they believed in various gods and assigned a deity for everything. For instance, Odin was the god of death, Thor was the god of thunder, and Loki was the god of mischief. There were about 66 gods and goddesses the Germanic people believed in. Like in most similar religions, there was also a god who served as the head of all other deities, and Odin filled this role. He was married to the goddess of fertility, Frigg, who became the chief goddess after marrying Odin. They had twin sons, Hodr and Baldur. Odin is believed to have married other goddesses and had many affairs with various other goddesses and giantesses as well, resulting in many children like Thor (the god of thunder), Heimdall (the watcher of Asgard, where the Norse gods reside), Vidar (god of revenge), Bragi (g0d of poetry), Hermodr (messenger 0f the gods), Tyr (the bravest of all gods), and many others. However, unlike in the Marvel movies, Loki wasn't Odin's son; he was a companion to some gods, including Odin and Thor.

The gods weren't represented as perfect beings, but they possessed various human qualities, and some of them were not exactly good, like Loki. To better understand Norse mythology and its various deities, let's look at some of its popular myths.

The Myth of the Death of Baldur

Baldur was the son of Odin and his wife, Frigg. He was very popular, loved, and respected among all the gods. His popularity resulted from his generosity, courage, and joyful personality. Everyone loved spending time with him. Baldur began having nightmares of something terrible befalling him. Many ancient cultures believed that their dreams held meaning back then. As a result, Baldur grew wary and turned to other gods, including his father Odin, to find the meaning behind these dreams.

Odin, concerned about his son, disguised himself and traveled to the underworld to seek the help of a dead seeress. A seeress is a woman who can perform sorcery and foretell the future. The seeress that Odin sought was known for her wisdom and dream interpretation. Upon his arrival at the underworld, Odin noticed that there were decorations and preparations held for a feast. Odin was bewildered and went to the seeress to inquire about the reason behind the festivity. The seeress had no idea that she was talking to the chief god and told him the festivity was held in Baldur's honor. However, this event would not end happily. She informed him that Baldur would meet his demise this evening during these festivities. Suddenly, the seeress fell silent and stopped herself from giving any more information because she realized the man she spoke to was none other than Odin.

Odin was heartbroken over the fate that would befall his son, and he went back to Asgard and shared this information with the other gods. When Frigg learned about the fate that awaited her son, she decided to do everything she could to save him. She went to every living and non-living entity in the universe and made them take an oath to never harm her son. Nothing and no one could touch Baldur now. Even when other gods, in jest, threw rocks at Baldur, he remained unharmed. Neither the rocks nor anyone or anything was breaking their oath.

Loki, who thrived on chaos and mischief, went to Frigg disguised as a woman to find out if all entities had taken the oath not to harm Baldur. Frigg told him that only the mistletoe hadn't taken an oath because it was so small and harmless, and she didn't believe it could hurt her son. Loki found a great opportunity to get rid of Baldur, who he was jealous of. This could have been the result of Baldur's popularity or because Loki enjoyed messing with the gods and watching everyone suffer.

The god of mischief carved a spear out of mistletoe and went to the place where the gods played around with Baldur. They threw things at him so they could see what could hurt him. Hodr, Baldur's twin brother, was blind and couldn't participate in these games. Loki convinced him that he should join the fun. It was also an honor to prove to Baldur how invincible he was. Loki offered to help Hodr to throw the spear in the right direction. Not knowing he was being tricked, Hodr threw the mistletoe spear at his brother, who met his demise on the spot.

This was a terrible incident that left all the gods speechless. They considered the death of Baldur as a sign that would bring about Ragnarok, or the end of the universe. Nana, Baldur's wife, couldn't handle the grief and died during her husband's funeral and was laid to rest by his side. Frigg was understandably heartbroken, but she composed herself to try to find a loyal and brave god who could travel to the underworld and meet the goddess of death, Hel, Loki's daughter. Frigg wanted to offer Hel a reward to bring Baldur and his wife back. Hermod, one of Odin's many sons, offered to take the journey.

Hermod traveled for nine nights until he reached the underworld and met with Hel. He found Baldur sitting next to Hel in the seat of honor. However, he wasn't his cheerful self; he was pale and downcast. Hermod begged Hel to bring his brother back to the land of the living. He told her how all living beings and gods were grieving over Baldur's death. She told him to prove that everyone was indeed mourning him. Hel promised him that if every being in the universe wept for Baldur, she would bring him back to life. However, Baldur would remain in the underworld if one creature didn't.

Hermod carried the message back, and the gods sent word across the cosmos. Everyone and everything wept for Baldur except Tokk, the giantess. You may have guessed it. This wasn't a real giantess, but Loki disguised as one to prevent Baldur from returning. His plan succeeded and Baldur's light was gone forever, condemned to spend eternity in the cold and dark underworld.

What Loki did couldn't go unpunished. He knew the gods were angry and were coming for him. He escaped and shapeshifted into some salmon, but Odin found him and informed the gods of his location. Loki was very intelligent, and the gods struggled to catch him as he kept shapeshifting and hiding in the sea. However, after many failed tries, Thor managed to catch Loki. The gods bound him in a cave and left a serpent above him, dripping venom over his face. Loki's screams were so loud that they shook the earth. He remained in the cave until Ragnarok.

The Myth of Ragnarok

If you watch Marvel movies, this name probably sounds familiar. Ragnarok was featured in one of Thor's movies. Although the story was portrayed in a light tone, the myth behind it is much darker. If the Viking's stories were chapters, the myth of Ragnarok should be the one closing the book since it foretold the end of the universe. The word Ragnarok means "the fate of the gods." The Vikings believed that Ragnarok would happen sometime in the future.

One day, the Norns (female beings who controlled the fate of the gods and mankind and who were even more powerful than all the gods, including Odin) will enforce a great winter. It will be different from any winter the world has ever seen. There will be snow coming from all directions, biting wind, and freezing cold. This winter will be longer than any other winter lasting for about a year without experiencing the warmth of the spring or the summer heat. As a result, the Earth will perish, and people will struggle to find food. They will have no choice but to forgo their morals and break the law to fight for their survival. Families will turn against each other and use their weapons instead of their tongues. Fathers will kill their sons, and brothers will murder each other.

Skoll and Hati, two mythical wolves who spent their time pursuing the sun and the moon, will achieve their goal during Ragnarok and devour the sun and the moon. The stars will also disappear, leaving the skies and the world void and dark. The mighty tree Yggdrasil that holds the cosmos together will tremble and will cause the collapse of all the mountains and the trees. Fenrir, a monstrous wolf and Loki's son (whom the gods have chained), will break free and wreak havoc. His mouth is huge, and he will run around devouring everything and everyone in his way. His brother Jormungandr, the serpent who resides at the bottom of the ocean, will rise and flood the Earth. He will use his venom to poison the Earth's air, land, and water. Then comes Naglfar, which is a ship made from the nails of the dead and whose crew are all giants, and its captain, the god of mischief himself, Loki. According to the myth, Loki will break free from his cave during Ragnarok and join his crew on Naglfar. They will sail and destroy everything in their way.

The sky will split open, paving the way to Muspelheim, a mythical world where giants made of fire reside. Their leader will have swords brighter than the sun. He and his people will come to Asgard through Bitforst (a rainbow bridge guarded by Heimdall. It connects to Midgard, the world where mankind resides). The people of Muspelheim will destroy the bridge. Heimdall will warn the gods that the moment they have been dreading has arrived. The gods are determined to not go down without a fight and will prepare to face the invaders. Their actions show extreme courage and bravery since they know from various prophecies that the battle will not end in their favor.

With the help of the spirits of all the soldiers in Valhalla, Odin will face Fenrir. Odin and his soldiers will fight with everything they have, but, unfortunately, they will be no match to Fenrir, who will devour them all. Odin's son Vidar will go after Fenrir to avenge his father. He will be wearing a shoe that was made for this very moment. Vidar will succeed and kill Fenrir. Loki and Heimdall will fight to the death as both gods will kill each other. Freyr, the god of peace and one of the most beloved gods in Norse mythology, will kill the leader of the Muspelheim. Thor will fight Jormungandr and kill him with his hammer but not before he spits his venom over Thor, leaving him to die moments later. Whatever and whoever is left after this battle will sink into the sea. The world will be empty as if it was never occupied by gods or mankind. To paraphrase the famous words by T.S. Eliot, this is the way the world ends, not with a bang but with Ragnarok.

Although many believed this was the end of this myth, others believed that this was merely the beginning. Not all the gods will fall. Hodr, Vali, Vidar, and Thor's sons Modi and Magni will survive. A man and a woman hidden during Ragnarok will emerge and act as Adam and Eve and populate the world. The sun's daughter will shine and light the skies.

The Myth of Thor's Hammer

If you are interested in comic books and Marvel movies, you are probably curious about the origins of Thor's hammer. Well, this story begins with none other than Loki. Thor was married to the goddess of fertility, Sif, who was famous for her long and beautiful golden hair. One day, Loki felt more mischievous than usual and decided to cut Sif's hair off. Thor fumed with rage, and he captured Loki and told him that he would break every bone in his body. Loki begged Thor to spare his life, and he offered to go to the home of the dwarves to ask them to craft a new head of hair for Sif that would be marvelous and more beautiful than her old hair. Thor agreed to let Loki go, and, for once, he kept his word. He convinced the dwarves to craft a new head of hair for Sif.

Loki decided to stay with the dwarves and caused chaos there as well. He challenged the two to create something unique and better than the other dwarves. He even bet his head that they would not be able to create anything special. Loki shapeshifted into a fly and taunted the two dwarves as they worked. One of the dwarves, Sindri, created a hammer, unlike anything anyone had ever seen. Once thrown, the hammer would always hit its target, never miss, and then fly back to its owner. However, nothing is perfect, and the hammer had one flaw: *its handle was too short*. Sindri named the hammer Mjollnir, which means lightning.

Loki took what the two dwarves crafted, including the hair and Mjollnir, and gave them as gifts to the gods. Sif was the recipient of the hair, and Thor was given Mjollnir. The gods appreciated the gifts but reminded Loki that he lost the bet and therefore owed the dwarves his head. When the dwarves came to collect, Loki, the ever so cunning god, told them that he bet his head and not his neck. The two dwarves then decided to sow Loki's mouth shut.

The Myth of Odin and the Runes

Now we come to the most important legend in this chapter: the runes' discovery. In Norse mythology, the runes are considered the language of the gods. In fact, we can't talk about Norse mythology without mentioning the runes because they played a big role in the mythology. Odin had always sought knowledge and wisdom. He even sacrificed his eyes to drink water from a well that would grant him knowledge of everything. Before the Latin alphabet became widely used, the Norse and Germanics relied on letters referred to as the runes. However, the runes weren't alphabets like the Latins, but they were symbols. These symbols were very powerful, and Odin was adamant about uncovering their secrets.

The Norns used the runes to shape the fate of the gods and mankind by engraving these symbols on Yggdrasil. Odin wanted this power for himself and wanted to learn about the mysteries of the runes. However, these symbols didn't reveal themselves to anyone unless they deemed themselves worthy of such power. Odin, who never hesitated to make a sacrifice for the sake of knowledge, hung himself from a Yggdrasi's branch and pierced himself with a spear. He remained in this position while looking downward at the water below. He made it clear to all the gods that they shouldn't rescue him. After nine days, the runes finally accepted Odin's sacrifice and began uncovering their mysteries to him. Odin began seeing the symbols of the runes, and all the knowledge behind them was revealed to him. This knowledge made Odin one of the most powerful beings in the universe and allowed him to help himself and his friends and vanquish his enemies.

There is no wonder that Norse mythology is extremely popular to this day. It is filled with fascinating tales about various gods and goddesses. The Vikings humanized their gods by giving them strengths and weaknesses instead of creating a perfect image of the divine. They also experienced human emotions like anger, pain, loss, and envy. With Ragnarok, the story of how the world ends, the Vikings depicted their gods as heroes who were willing to fight even when they knew they would lose and perish. This is quite similar to the traits of the Viking soldiers, who were known to be brave and fierce warriors.

Now that you have become familiar with Norse mythology, you are ready to uncover the secrets behind the runes.

Chapter 2: The History of the Runes

In the previous chapter, we discussed how Odin's thirst for knowledge led him to uncover the secrets of the runes. Odin, one of the most powerful gods in the universe, had to hang himself to appease the Norns so he could uncover the mysteries of the runes. Was his sacrifice necessary? Are the runes that important? What exactly were the runes? These are all the questions we will cover in this chapter.

What Are Runes?

The runes are a reading system but were regarded as *much more*. They were considered a gift from the divine, and indeed they were. Odin sacrificed himself to learn about the runes and give their knowledge to mankind. Although the runes acted as letters the Norse people used to communicate with each other, they were different from the letters we are accustomed to today. A rune is a pictographic symbol of cosmological power. When you write down a rune, you aren't just writing a letter or drawing a symbol; you are invoking the power behind it. The runes gave the Germanic people answers to life's most complicated questions and helped them look at situations from a different and more insightful perspective.

The word rune has a different meaning in many languages. For example, in Old Norse, it means "mysteries," in Old Irish, it means "secret," in Old English, it means "whisper; in Middle Welsh, it means "magic charm," in Finnish, it means "chant" or "song," and in Icelandic, it means "friend." Before the word "runes" referred to the Norse alphabet, it used to mean a "hushed message." Many of these translations are quite appropriate descriptions of the runes since they were, in fact, a secret language until Odin uncovered their secrets.

Unlike how alphabets were written over the centuries using ink and paper, the Norse people carved the runes on hard surfaces like wood, metal, or stone.

The Norse and Germanic people believed that the runes were magic. They even engraved them on their jewelry, weapons, and amulets to give them power. For this reason, they didn't just use the runes as a regular alphabet for writing and communication. Like Odin, they also believed in the metaphysical power behind the runes' symbols. The Norse people took advantage of this power to help them communicate with the supernatural world and incorporated them into different incantations.

Since the runes were considered divine and enchanting, they were connected to the names of various Norse gods. For instance, the rune Thurs is associated with Thor, and the rune Tyr is associated with Tyr, the god of war.

How the Germanic People Used the Runes

It is believed that the Germanic people used the runes from 160 AD to 1500 AD. Instead of using them to simply communicate with one another, the Vikings used the rune symbols according to the powers they invoked. For example, they uncovered their secrets and used them to predict the future, marked their fallen heroes' graves with the runes' symbols, and they also used them to honor their ancestors. There are also rune inscriptions on buildings, bricks, cliff walls, crafts, art, religious objects, magical charms, and weapons.

The boulders the Vikings used to honor their dead are called runestones. There are thousands of rune-stones in Scandinavia, and historians estimate that there are over 3000 of them. The Vikings needed big rocks to commemorate their dead as sometimes they would inscribe a whole poem for them. One of the most popular runestones that featured a poem was the Kjula Runestone which was about the fall of a man called Spear. During the Viking era, the runestones were usually found near graves. They are usually found in Denmark and Norway, but most are in Sweden.

Although some people believed that the runes could predict the future, others believed that they could give them an idea of what the future held and help them find solutions to their problems. The runes merely offered suggestions of what a person should do in case a certain event took place. Simply put, they gave people hints of how they should act, but the rest was up to them. They were free to make their own decisions or let their intuition guide them.

The Vikings believed in free will, so when the runes suggested something about the future, they didn't treat it as something fixed. They believed that they could change the outcome if they made different decisions. The Norse people appreciated the rune guidance as it helped them see the bigger picture in various situations and provided them with more information to make better decisions.

Later, the Vikings began using the rune alphabets for communications. In fact, we have believed for centuries that the runes were only used on religious objects and to commemorate the dead. However, in the 1950s, excavators discovered in Norway that the Vikings used the runes like regular alphabets for correspondence and business. Just think of how we use letters now. The Vikings used the runes for the same purposes. Whether they wrote jokes, sent love letters, inscribed prayers, or sent personal messages, the runes were a big part of how the Germanic people communicated with each other.

The History of the Runes

The fascination with runes isn't something new. Since they were featured in J.R.R. Tolkien's "Lord of the Rings," people have been curious about them and their origins. The Northern Germanic people were the ones that created the runic symbols in 100 A.D. Historians believe that when the Germanic people raided places near the Mediterranean, they were influenced by the ancient Roman alphabet. However, others argue that they were influenced by the Etruscan letters.

When runes were first discovered, they were only used for inscriptions. Archeologists found runic inscriptions on a Vimose comb in Denmark that they believed to have dated back to 160 A.D. Runes were a huge part of Norse mythology since the Norse people used them to memorialize their main historical events like their wars and stories of their gods.

Although only the Norse and Germanic people used the runes, inscriptions are found in countries like England, Greece, Russia,

Greenland, and Turkey. The Viking travelers didn't use any other alphabets, so they would inscribe the runes wherever they went on journeys or when they conquered a new country.

The Vikings used the runes for over 3000 years until the Middle Ages. By then, Latin alphabets were taking over the world, and the use of the runes had died out. However, as mentioned, they are still used in modern literature.

In the 20th century, Nazis started using runes again. They were responsible for spreading confusion and portraying the runes negatively. They believed that the runes were the first alphabet known to man. However, this wasn't true as various cultures had their own alphabets well before the runes came into being. They modified them and started using them, which led to the spread of misinformation surrounding these symbols. For instance, the swastika, considered a sacred symbol during the Viking era, became associated with the Nazis. Luckily, authors like J.R.R. Tolkien and J.K. Rowling gave a new life to the runes and made people curious about their origin so they could discover that they were enchanting symbols that didn't have any evil or racist roots.

The Runes in Literature

We mentioned how Odin wanted the power of the runes all to himself. Indeed, he always sought knowledge and wisdom. However, he was also jealous of the Norns and how they could control everyone's fate by using the power and knowledge of the runes. The story of Odin's jealousy and sacrifice was mentioned in the poem Hávamál, which translates to "Sayings of the High One," referring to Odin. This poem is a part of the Poetic Eddas, which are collections of anonymous Old Norse poems. Still, if it wasn't for Odin's sacrifice, it is believed that mankind would never have been able to learn about the runes or their power and magic. Odin was the one who gave the world the knowledge of the runes. However, he knew how powerful and mighty they were, so he kept some of the most powerful ones to himself and shared the others with mankind. This is another proof of Odin's wisdom as he knew men couldn't handle such power as, in most cases, it would corrupt them.

The runes were heavily featured in literature, especially in poetry. The Norse and Germanics, like many other ancient cultures, didn't record their tales in writing but passed them down orally. Many of the runic poems passed down to us were written after Christianity spread through

Europe, and pagan ideas were no longer welcomed. For this reason, the runes went through various interpretations. Small verses in Norse, Icelandic, and Old English literature explain the meaning behind the runes. However, these verses were written after the runic lore was lost, which is why some of these poems seem to contradict each another and can be confusing. Additionally, runes were used in various Scandinavian countries, and we believe that they didn't share the same meanings.

The Runic Alphabets in Germanic Cultures

Although we refer to them as runic alphabets, the runic system is called Futhark runes. This name was chosen to avoid confusion. The word alphabet comes from the words "alpha" and "beta," the first two letters in the Greek alphabet. Unlike the alphabets we use now, the runes didn't start with the letters A and B, which is why the scholars opted for Futhark instead.

Like the Latin alphabet's strong connection with Christianity, nobility, and Catholic scholars, the Futhark runes played a huge role in the Norse religion. They were used in various rituals, and, until this day, runic inscriptions can be found on church walls. Runes and their religious connection should come as no surprise since they were considered divine as they came from Odin.

Several runic letters and inscriptions discovered gave us an idea of how the Germanic people lived their daily lives. For instance, the word "*litiluism*" was found carved on a ship which translates to "man knows little." This can reflect the wisdom of the people back then and how they were aware that they didn't know everything and that there was still much they needed to learn. There was also an inscription found in Gol Stave Church in Norway that says, "*Kyss á mik, þvíat ek erfiða,*" which translates to "kiss me because I am troubled." This saying is believed to refer to a saint who was hung there. There were also rune inscriptions on various things to declare ownership. For instance, women would engrave their names and the runic word for "own" on their buckets.

The Vikings weren't just warriors. Love and romance were a part of their culture as well. Runic alphabets were used to send sweet and romantic messages, albeit using some of the strangest methods. For instance, on the bones of a cow, this sentence was engraved "*kyss mik,*" which means "kiss me." On another bone, the words "*Óst min, kyss mik*" were engraved, meaning "my love, kiss me." They also used the rune letters to write love poems, usually inscribed on rune sticks.

Rune letters were also used in businesses. Tradesmen often sent inscribed rune sticks of the merchandise they sent to other merchants. For instance, they would engrave the merchant's name and add the products they were selling, like "Merchant (name) is sending you salt." There were also engravings and short inscriptions on jewelry, especially that worn by dead women. The exact meanings behind these inscriptions remain a mystery as they are hard to translate. However, they may have been the jewelry owners' names or their makers.

The written word has always been associated with news and gossip. Rune letters are no different. Engravings were found that indicate the Germanic people used runes to spread idle gossip. The Vikings also used to engrave their weapons, but there are still debates on what these engravings mean. They are either the names of the weapon's owners or their makers. They could also be the characteristics or the names of the weapon itself. For instance, one of the weapons had the rune word for "black" engraved on it. This could be either the owner's name, the maker, or the weapon's description. There were engravings found on shields as well. These engravings indicate that the soldiers and the silversmith were literate.

There is a misconception among many people that the Vikings didn't know how to read. This is probably the result of how they are usually depicted in movies or TV shows as savages who only care about fighting or conquering other countries. However, from everything we have learned so far and the existence and popularity of the runes back in the day, it is quite obvious that the Vikings were anything but illiterate. They understood and used the runes in their everyday lives. The biggest proof that they could read the runes is the thousands of runestones that were found all over Scandinavia. However, some scholars believed that the Vikings could only read and understand the runes at a basic level. The Vikings believed that only the gods could understand the wisdom behind them.

Although the Germanics used the runes mainly in their Scandinavian language, later, they began using them to write in other languages as well. A few inscriptions were found where the Germanics used the runes to write Latin text, and there were also a couple of occasions where they used the runes to write in English.

Runes in Norse Magic and Divination

During the Viking era, words weren't so easily uttered. One couldn't say a word and then go back on it. Words held extreme power. The way people pronounced each word could directly influence their lives. Once a sentence is spoken out loud, it can greatly impact a person's life. It is out there in the universe, and no power can take it back. Reality can't influence words. In fact, words hold the power to create reality. Words are thoughts. Can you think without using words or language? Languages influence our perception of the world around us. The Vikings believed that once you transformed your thoughts into words, they could, to some degree, alter reality.

Various linguists believe there is a connection between the meaning of a word and the sound it makes. Simply put, the sound carries the word's meaning. The same is applied to the runes, where each word's sound is connected to its meaning. However, as mentioned, runes are symbols, which adds another layer to this theory. There is also a connection between the shape of the rune and the sound it makes.

Therefore, the runes weren't just used to communicate in the physical world. These symbols were powerful enough to be used to communicate with non-human beings and to reach out to the supernatural world as well. For this reason, they can be used while performing magical spells. We mentioned how the Norns used the runes' power to alter the fate of the gods and mankind. Most people use magic to change their fate. They either want to become rich, fall in love, or cure the sick. Magic is all about rewriting one's story so you can change the course of your life.

As a result of its impact on one's fate, the Germanics found that at their core, runes were magic. That said, scholars often have debates on this topic. Some believe that even though rune symbols have been used in various spells, that doesn't mean that they are magical in nature. However, the Vikings may disagree with Egil's Saga, which depicted the life of the Egill Skallagrímsson clan. One day, Egil, a Viking poet, was traveling. He met a Viking farmer who invited Egil to share a meal with him. The farmer had a very sick daughter, so he asked Egil to help him find a remedy for her. As Egil was examining the girl, he found an unexpected surprise. There was a whale bone in the girl's bed with runic inscriptions.

When Egil asked the girl's father about the bone, he told him another farmer's son had engraved these runes; he said the boy was illiterate and most likely had no idea what these inscriptions meant. This was true as the boy only wanted the farmer's daughter to fall in love with him. However, since he didn't understand the meaning behind the symbols, he used the wrong ones and made the girl sick. Unlike the young boy, Egil was an expert. He told the father that these inscriptions were what made his daughter ill. Egil took the bone and destroyed it with fire. He wrote a new inscription using different runes from the ones the young farmer boy used. This was meant to reverse the malice from the whalebone inscriptions. The new runes worked their magic, and the girl recovered quickly. This means that not only were the runes used for spells, but the Nordic people believed the symbols themselves were magic.

This story proves that Norse people believed in the magical powers behind the runes. They understood that these symbols were strong enough to make someone extremely sick and help them easily recover. They didn't just use the runes' magical power in inscriptions. These symbols were also used in various spells and magical formulas. Runes were also used for protection spells, finding love, curing the sick, and everything else. However, one must understand the meaning behind each rune symbol before attempting to use them, or they can backfire, as we have learned from the farmer's daughter's story.

Odin also used the rune magic. He had a spear called Gungnir, engraved with magical runic symbols, and these symbols gave Gungnir magical powers. Just like Thor's hammer, Mjölnir, Gungnir was also crafted by dwarves and could always hit its target without fail.

The Germanic people took advantage of the relationship between the rune meaning and its phonetic sound to perform divination so they could foretell the future. In Norse mythology, practitioners who performed divination were able to foresee the future so they could alter their fate. When Vikings gained experience in using the runes, they used what they learned to practice divination. We understand that the runes were a vital tool the Vikings used in divination. However, we don't know how they used them as this information never got as far as us. Odin's main purpose behind sharing the runes with mankind was magic. He had no interest in people using them for communication.

As mentioned, some believe that the runes aren't magical. They are letters like all the others used in different languages. However, they can still be used in spells. Similar to how we use our alphabet to write or create a spell, the runes can be used in the same way, just like in Harry Potter, where they used the word "Lumos" to light the tip of a wand, using the rune's letters together can create magical words and spells. Runes can be used to create a charm or a spell and engrave it onto an amulet to protect its wearer, heal them, or alter their fate.

For instance, the inscription "healing runes I cut, runes of help" was discovered in Sweden. This charm was used to treat and heal the sick, and it was never specified how they were supposed to heal or what their functions were. The Germanic people clearly believed that the runes were powerful enough and could indeed heal.

To learn about a culture, you should first learn its language. When archaeologists discovered engraved rocks, walls, runestones, etc., they gained insight into the Vikings and learned about different aspects of their lives. This study taught us about the lives of gods, kings, and peasants. The runes and their magical powers made us feel connected with the Nordic people as we can relate to them and their struggles. By learning about the spells they cast, the names of the people they often engraved for various spells, or even the name of the object's makers, we are no longer reading about anonymous people. We are learning about specific individuals with whom we can connect, feel their pain, and sympathize with what they were going through. Runes aren't just powerful because they possess magic and knowledge. They are a language that an entire culture used for 3000 years to create a civilization with fascinating tales and mythology that we are still studying to this day.

Now you have learned about the history of the runes, you are ready to dive in and learn about Elder's Futhark runes and the meaning of each letter in the alphabet.

Chapter 3: The Runic Alphabet

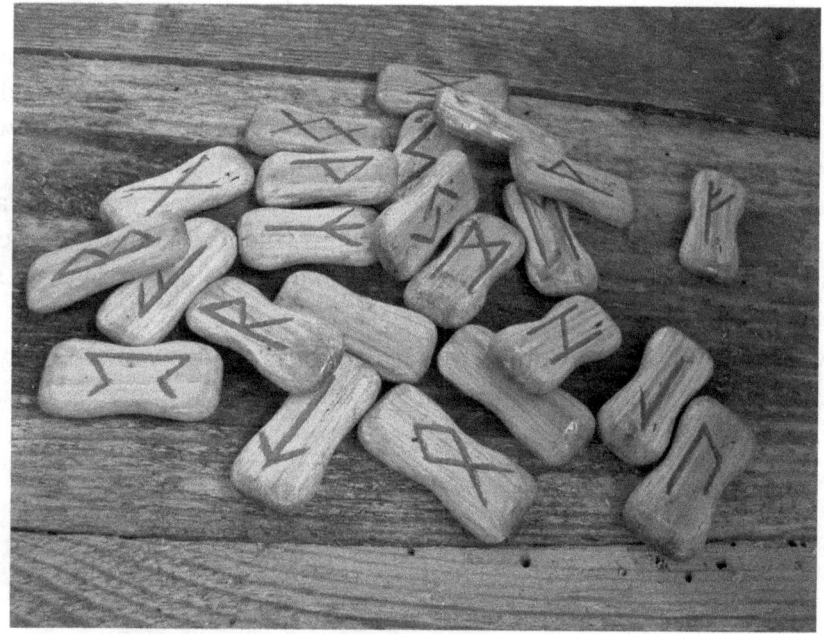

Runes on wood.
https://pixabay.com/images/id-947831/

As you know by now, Odin discovered the runic alphabet after hanging from the Yggdrasil (the World Tree) for nine days. Following this, the runes became available to mankind - beginning with Northern Europe. There is evidence of the runic alphabet on fragments of stone, bark, and bone found in Norse archeological sites - along with other remnants of the ancient Norse culture. With this chapter, you will have a chance to learn how the runes, the archaic Norse language of symbols, make up an alphabet called the Futhark.

While the runic alphabet is rarely used as a language in modern times, learning how to use it even to translate simple texts can help you understand their role in divinations, spellcasting, gridwork, and much more. To help you start your journey, this chapter will also provide tips on how to practice translating texts from modern English to Elder Futhark. In the beginning, it may sound complicated, but after you learn how to write using the runes, you will realize how much they can enhance your practice.

What Is the Runic Alphabet?

The runic alphabet is made up of several runes that create a written language when used together. Several types of runic alphabets are left over from different regions and periods throughout history. The ones that enjoyed widespread and long-standing use include:

- The Elder Futhark (used from the 2nd to the 8th century)
- The Younger Futhark (used from the 8th to the 9th century)
- Anglo-Saxon Futhorc (used from the 5th to 11th century)
- The Medieval Futhark (used from the 12th to the 15th century)
- Dalecarlian runes (used from the 16th to the 19th century)
- Gothic Runes (used from an unknown time to the 4th century)
- Turkic (Orkhon) Script (used from the 8th to the 9th century)
- Old Hungarian Script (used from the 8th to the 11th century)

The oldest one of these is believed to be the Elder Futhark, which is where the name of the runic alphabet (Futhark) comes from. From about 200-800 AD, the Elder Futhark alphabet, a set of 24 runes, was used for writing throughout the Scandinavian region and other parts of Northern Europe. "Futhark" is a word derived from the first six letters of the alphabet, which are "Fehu," "Uruz," "Thurisaz," "Ansuz," "Raidho," and "Kenaz." The 24 letters of the Elder Futhark were divided into three groups called ættir. The first runes of each ættir (Fehu, Hagalaz, and Tiwaz) are also called the Mother Runes because they're believed to be the first runes added to the Elder Futhark alphabet – and all the others in the group – can be tied to them phonetically. This is crucial information as the entire alphabet is based on a phonetic system rather than written forms.

Nowadays, Elder Futhark is typically used to provide background for a better understanding of the Younger Futhark, the alphabet of the Viking Age - which was the successor of the Elder Futhark. Around the end of the 8th century, the Futhark was shortened to 16 runes, and the Younger Futhark was born. The shape of the runic alphabet symbols has also changed. The runic letters have become simpler - with each rune having only one vertical mark called "stave." Vikings found it easier to carve the letters of their new alphabet. They could swiftly move on to more important matters after finishing what they needed to mark down. The runes of the Younger Futhark alphabet are carved with full or long vertical strokes - whereas Elder Futhark often requires three or more strokes per rune.

The Complete List of Elder Futhark Runes

Unlike the letters in modern alphabets, the letters in the runic alphabet have meanings tied to natural forces. And just as nature goes through endless cycles of change, these universal forces also change and evolve with time. And while the runic language doesn't have widespread use nowadays, the meaning of its letters is just as relevant today as they were thousands of years ago. Here is what each rune in the Elder Futhark alphabet means in modern English, alongside their phonetic equivalent and modern pronunciation.

Fehu

- **Symbol:** ᚠ
- **Phonetic Value:** F
- **English Pronunciation:** "FAY-hoo"
- **Translation:** Cattle, prosperity, property, hope, happiness, abundance, wealth, and financial gain.

Uruz

- **Symbol:** ᚢ
- **Phonetic Value:** U
- **English Pronunciation:** "OO-rooz"

- **Translation:** Wild ox, unexpected change, life force, indomitability, strength, power, and good mental and physical health.

Thurisaz

- **Symbol:** Þ
- **Phonetic Value:** Th
- **English Pronunciation:** "THUR-ee-sazh"
- **Translation:** Giant, god of Thunder, lightning, thorn, caution, defensive force, and disruption.

Ansuz

- **Symbol:** F
- **Phonetic Value:** A
- **English Pronunciation:** "AHHN-sooz"
- **Translation:** Wisdom, mouth, listening, breathing, prophecies, communication, and Odin and the ancestral gods.

Raidho

- **Symbol:** R
- **Phonetic Value:** R
- **English Pronunciation:** "Ra-EED-ho"
- **Translation:** Travel, rest, rhythm, journey, the big picture, change, and momentum.

Kenaz

- **Symbol:** <
- **Phonetic Value:** C / K
- **English Pronunciation:** "KEN-aahz"
- **Translation:** Controlled energy, torch, fire, passion, light, creation, beacon, and transformation.

Gebo

- **Symbol:** X
- **Phonetic Value:** G
- **English Pronunciation:** "GHEB-o"
- **Translation:** Gratitude, gift, generosity, exchange, unity, receiving, self-sacrifice, forgiveness, and offering.

Wunjo

- **Symbol:** ᚹ
- **Phonetic Value:** W
- **English Pronunciation:** "WOON-yo"
- **Translation:** Satisfaction, euphoria, fulfillment, well-being, happiness, self-alignment, harmony, and joy.

Haglaz

- **Symbol:** H
- **Phonetic Value:** H
- **English Pronunciation:** "HA-ga-lahz"
- **Translation:** Hail, destruction, sudden difficulties, violent change of nature, and delay.

Naudiz

- **Symbol:** ᛏ
- **Phonetic Value:** N
- **English Pronunciation:** "NOWD-heez"
- **Translation:** Need, distress, desire for triumph, stagnation, and change manifestation.

Isa

- **Symbol:** I
- **Phonetic Value:** I
- **English Pronunciation:** "EE-sa"

- **Translation:** Stillness, cold, ice, winter, postponement, delay, and forced pause before a new beginning.

Jera

- **Symbol:** ᚼ
- **Phonetic Value:** J / Y
- **English Pronunciation:** "YAIR-ah"
- **Translation:** Nature's cycle, harvest, rewards for efforts, movement in time, and reaping what you've sown.

Eihwaz

- **Symbol:** ᛇ
- **Phonetic Value:** E / I
- **English Pronunciation:** "EYE-wahz"
- **Translation:** Longevity, wisdom, death, renewal, Yew tree, life, sacrifice, and passing through a gateway.

Perthro

- **Symbol:** ᛈ
- **Phonetic Value:** P
- **English Pronunciation:** "PER-thro"
- **Translation:** Mystery, hidden desires, fate, divination, casting, secret, and the quest for self-knowledge.

Algiz

- **Symbol:** ᛉ
- **Phonetic Value:** Z
- **English Pronunciation:** "Ahl-geez"
- **Translation:** Instinct, sanctuary, elk, luck, connection to the higher self, good omen, and protection.

Sowilo

- **Symbol:** ᛊ
- **Phonetic Value:** S
- **English Pronunciation:** "So-WEE-lo"
- **Translation:** Health, vitality, good energy, enlightenment, spiritual power, success, personal growth, and sun.

Tiwaz

- **Symbol:** ᛏ
- **Phonetic Value:** T
- **English Pronunciation:** "TEE-wahz"
- **Translation:** The God Tyr, victory, bravery, courage, need for justice, honor, and sacrifice for the greater good.

Berkano

- **Symbol:** ᛒ
- **Phonetic Value:** B
- **English Pronunciation:** "BER-kah-no"
- **Translation:** Rebirth, new beginnings, relationship, project, life cycle, and birch tree.

Ehwaz

- **Symbol:** ᛖ
- **Phonetic Value:** E
- **English Pronunciation:** "EH-waz"
- **Translation:** Loyalty, cooperation, movement, forward progress, horse, and partnership.

Mannaz

- **Symbol:** ᛗ
- **Phonetic Value:** M
- **English Pronunciation:** "MAN-naz"

- **Translation:** Balance, intelligence, reason, divine potential, tradition, talent development, and humanity.

Laguz

- **Symbol:** ᛚ
- **Phonetic Value:** L
- **English Pronunciation:** "LAH-good"
- **Translation:** Water, intuition, flow, cleansing, inward journey, personality depth.

Ingwaz

- **Symbol:** ᛜ
- **Phonetic Value:** Ng
- **English Pronunciation:** "ING-waz"
- **Translation:** Inner growth, male sexuality, potential energy, family lines, perfect timing, ancestry, and fertility.

Dagaz

- **Symbol:** ᛞ
- **Phonetic Value:** D
- **English Pronunciation:** "DAH-gahz"
- **Translation:** The light of the gods, sudden change, awakening, day, enlightenment, inspiration, and self-transformation.

Othala

- **Symbol:** ᛟ
- **Phonetic Value:** O
- **English Pronunciation:** "OH-the-la"
- **Translation:** Spirituality, ancestral property, wisdom, belonging, homecoming, community, and inherent talent.

How Does the Runic Alphabet Compare to Modern Languages?

A phonetically perfect alphabet has a separate symbol (letter or rune) for each sound used in the language. As far as historical evidence shows, the Elder Futhark runic alphabet was like that. We know this because the Proto-Norse alphabet was developed after the Elder Futhark runes, and the former had the exact number of sounds as the former did. However, Roman letters used in the Modern English language are not even close to this ideal phonetic alphabet. There are many sounds without a letter of their own and can be transcribed only through letters or combinations of letters used for other sounds. A great example of this issue would be using sh for (ʃ) or ch for (tʃ).

The following table illustrates how the runic alphabet compares to the modern English, Norwegian, Swedish, and Danish alphabets.

Futhark	English	Norwegian	Swedish	Danish
ᚠ	A	A	A	A
ᛒ	B	B	B	B
ᛗ	D	D	D	D
ᛘ	E	E	E	E
ᚹ	F	F	F	F
ᚷ	G	G	G	G
ᚺ	H	H	H	H
ᛁ	I	I	I	I
ᛋ	J/Y	J	J	J

ᚲ	C/K	K	K	K
ᛚ	L	L	L	L
ᛗ	M	M	M	M
ᛏ	N	N	N	N
ᛜ	O	O	O	O
ᛖ	P	P	P	P
	Q	Q	Q	Q
ᛉ	R	R	R	R
ᛊ	S	S	S	S
↑	T	T	T	T
ᚾ	U	U	U	U
ᚹ	V/W	V	V	V
		W	W	W
		X	X	X
		Y	Y	Y
ᛦ	Z	Z	Z	Z
ᚦ	Th			

ʃ	E/I				
◊	Ng				
			Æ		Æ
			Ø		Ø
			Å	Å	Å
				Ä	
				Ö	

The runic alphabet is also often compared to the Proto-Norse language - the predecessor of the modern Nordic languages. Some even use Proto-Norse as an intermediary to translate the runic language. However, the phonological system (sound system) of the Proto-Norse language was different from in modern English. For instance, English has the sounds (dʒ), (tʃ), (ʒ), and (ʃ) - which don't exist in the Proto-Norse language. The Proto-Norse phonetic system can't be equated with the Elder Stark alphabet even though it originates from it.

The Anglo-Saxon (the predecessor of the modern English language) script added letters to the runic alphabet to represent sounds of Old English that did not occur in the Elder or Younger Futhark. To start with, Anglo-Saxon Futhark had 28 letters as opposed to the 24 in the Elder one, and after about 900 AD, it already had 33. To this day, Scandinavian languages are even richer in sounds than English. However, instead of adding letters to the Futhark to represent the new sounds, the Anglo-Saxon runic alphabet compounded started to use the same letter to represent more than one sound. For example, they started to use one letter for the phonetic versions of k and g.

In practice, the reduction of the Futhark to 16 letters means that if you don't have the context of the text, it's impossible to tell which sound was meant by a certain rune. On the other hand, as runes became obsolete, the languages were allowed to develop so that the runes were simply reused for a different sound.

ᚲ	C/K	K	K	K
ᛚ	L	L	L	L
ᛗ	M	M	M	M
ᛏ	N	N	N	N
ᛜ	O	O	O	O
ᛖ	P	P	P	P
	Q	Q	Q	Q
ᚱ	R	R	R	R
ᛋ	S	S	S	S
ᛏ	T	T	T	T
ᚢ	U	U	U	U
ᚹ	V/W	V	V	V
		W	W	W
		X	X	X
		Y	Y	Y
ᛉ	Z	Z	Z	Z
ᚦ	Th			

ʃ	E/I			
◊	Ng			
		Æ		Æ
		Ø		Ø
		Å	Å	Å
			Ä	
			Ö	

The runic alphabet is also often compared to the Proto-Norse language - the predecessor of the modern Nordic languages. Some even use Proto-Norse as an intermediary to translate the runic language. However, the phonological system (sound system) of the Proto-Norse language was different from in modern English. For instance, English has the sounds (dʒ), (tʃ), (ʒ), and (ʃ) - which don't exist in the Proto-Norse language. The Proto-Norse phonetic system can't be equated with the Elder Stark alphabet even though it originates from it.

The Anglo-Saxon (the predecessor of the modern English language) script added letters to the runic alphabet to represent sounds of Old English that did not occur in the Elder or Younger Futhark. To start with, Anglo-Saxon Futhark had 28 letters as opposed to the 24 in the Elder one, and after about 900 AD, it already had 33. To this day, Scandinavian languages are even richer in sounds than English. However, instead of adding letters to the Futhark to represent the new sounds, the Anglo-Saxon runic alphabet compounded started to use the same letter to represent more than one sound. For example, they started to use one letter for the phonetic versions of k and g.

In practice, the reduction of the Futhark to 16 letters means that if you don't have the context of the text, it's impossible to tell which sound was meant by a certain rune. On the other hand, as runes became obsolete, the languages were allowed to develop so that the runes were simply reused for a different sound.

Writing Modern Words in Runes

So, as you've seen throughout this chapter, writing modern words using the runic alphabet can be rather challenging. There is no runic outlet designed for contemporary languages - particularly not modern English. Elder Futhark has fewer runes than the 26-letter Roman alphabet used to write modern English. It also has far fewer symbols equivalent to the sounds we use today.

If you try to use the Elder Futhark runes phonetically, that would be substituting runes for the sounds you hear in a word. While the runic alphabet was supposed to be used this way, it won't work with modern English because - as mentioned before- there are not enough runes for all the English sounds. For example, if you would want to spell the word "horse," its rune equivalent as we hear it would be ᚺᛟᚱᛊ, which spells "*hors.*" On the other hand, if you write it as ᚺᛟᚱᛊᛖ, this will change its spelling in the running language. An even more complicated example is the word "knight." According to letters used in English, you would need to transcribe this word as ᚲᚾᛁᚷᚺᛏ, which, to anyone reading it, will sound nothing like the original word. The closest representation of this word phonetically would be ᚾᚨᛁᛏ, which is very different from the way the word is spelled in English.

So, the most convenient solution for transcribing to or from the runic alphabet is to keep the modern English spelling. This would be far easier than figuring out how to combine runes for the letter s and h for (ʃ) when they appear in words like "shame" or c and h for (tʃ) in "child." And it would definitely be a preferable option to dwell on which rune to use when there are 3 variants of the same sound, as is the case with (dʒ) in "joy," "edge," and "gin."

Another curious thing about the runic language is that the same runes were never repeated one after another, even if they appear that way in a word. This is because there weren't too many words like that in the ancient Norse languages. In fact, most of them appeared along with the anglicized version and under the influence of Latin languages. In modern English, for example, the letters c and k often appear one after another. Since the rune for both letters is the same, if you wanted to translate a word containing both, you would only use one rune instead of two. This shortens the word but may take some practice until you learn how to do it correctly because it often leads to confusion when you read it back.

There is also the issue of writing directions. Early evidence shows that there was no set direction to runic writing. Rune carvers would write from left to right or right to left, with some inscriptions combining the two methods. Others even used individual runes written as a mirror image of the main direction of the script. From the archeological evidence from the 11th century onwards, the direction of runic language seems to have been set to the now-familiar left to right. This was probably the result of the influence of Latin languages and is the direction used nowadays to translate modern languages into Elder Futhark runes.

Anglo-Saxon runes are unsuitable for writing Modern English because there are no letters for some sounds that did not exist in Old English. But you can "cheat" and use the late medieval Scandinavian runic alphabet, which has a rune for every letter in the basic Latin alphabet. You can simply substitute a rune for every letter in an English word without caring about the actual pronunciation of the word.

Or you could use runes to write Modern English, partly based on the modern orthography in Latin script but also to some extent on pronunciation. For example, you may use the ng-rune for the sound "ng" in "sing" instead of separating the letters and using the runes for "n" and "g." Typically, someone who wants to write modern English using one of the futharks will replace the English letters in a word with the rune (or combination of runes) that makes the same sound. It can be a little tricky depending on which Futhark is being used, as there isn't a 1:1 correspondence of sounds to characters, but it's usually possible to figure out a way to do it.

Practicing the Runic Alphabet

It's recommended to have the entire runic alphabet and its English equivalents printed or written out on a sheet of paper. Keep this sheet in front of you whenever you practice, thus avoiding wasting time going back and looking up a rune every time you forget which letter it corresponds to. Whether you print it or write it by hand, use block letters for the English as they are closer in their form to Elder Futhark than cursive, which makes them easier to remember.

To avoid any confusion, you should start practicing by translating a few simple English words. Then you can try simple sentences. By mastering them, you may slowly work toward more complicated texts. You can even start by writing your name - beginning with your first name and following up with your last name (and middle name if you have one). That said, even some of the simple names can lead to a bit of confusion when you read them back. If you remember the rule about avoiding repetition, you will understand why this may cause a problem. For instance, if your name is "Jack," you will write it as ᛊᚨᚲ, and not ᛊᚨᚲᚲ. Remember, when using the runic alphabet, you're not writing the words; you are transcribing their pronunciation.

If you have several repetitions in your name, you may want to start with another word instead. Either way, writing words phonetically will make much more sense for you, at least in the beginning. Here are a few simple sentences you can practice with:

I want to drink water. - ᛁ·ᚹᚨᛏ·ᛏᛟ·ᛞᚱᛁᛏᚲ·ᚹᚨᛏᛖᚱ

The bird sings, and I listen to it. - ᛏᚺᛖ·ᛒᛁᚱᛞ·ᛊᛁᛜᛋ·ᚨᛜᛞ·ᛁ·ᛚᛁᛊᛏᛖᛜ·ᛏᛟ·ᛁᛏ

The air is cold, and the water is frozen. - ᛏᚺᛖ·ᚠᛁᚱ·ᛁᛊ·cᛟᛚᛞ·ᚨᛜᛞ·ᛏᚺᛖ·ᚹᚨᛏᛖᚱ·ᛁᛊ·ᚠᚱᛟᛉᛖᛜ

Use the table above to find the rune equivalent for the letters, write them out, then check if you got them right.

While placing dots between the words is a debated practice, beginners often find it easier to use the dots to separate the symbols. This way, you can ensure that you leave enough room between the words, and you'll be able to read them later without getting confused about which rune belongs to which word. Speaking of reading, this practice should always accompany your writing. Anytime you practice writing a word or sentence, you should also practice reading it back. Move on to a different word only after you are confident in writing and reading the current one.

Having practiced using the simple use of the runic alphabet, you can move on to using bind runes. Bind runes are two runes written on top of each other to make a new one. During the time Elder Futhark was still used, these runes were used to transcribe names, much like the initials we use today. However, you can also use it to empower your magical practice with a rune you designed for that specific purpose. Whether you opt for sticking to the existing runes or creating your own, practicing them is essential to harness their energy. The more you familiarize yourself with each symbol by writing it down, the easier it will be to become connected with their energy.

Chapter 4: The Three Runic Aettir

After reading the previous chapter, you may have noticed that the runes of the Elder Futhark don't follow the same order as the letters of the Roman alphabet. This is because each *aett* is built on a foundation provided by the Mother Runes. These were the first runes of the aett, which were given to mankind by Odin. Every rune that follows them follows logical patterns dictated by the first one. This chapter discusses the three Aettir and their respective runes. It will provide information on the meaning of each aett and runes, as they all form part of life cycles - from birth to death to rebirth. You'll also find a meditation exercise where you can connect with the energy of each aett by focusing on the deities who rule them.

Freyr's Aett

Freyr is the Norse god of fertility who ruled over the first aett. Along with his goddess Freya, this deity represents a unity in which nature, kinships, marriages, and all other relationships prosper. The runes in this aett speak of what you need to achieve to fulfill your destiny. They represent experiences and interactions with your inner self, others, and the divine. They bring order to chaos just as the order was brought on when the universe was created. Freyr's aett contains the oldest runic symbols discovered so far, indicating the beginning of life and the birth of a new culture. From symbolizing survival of this birth to the realization of happiness, these runes empower you in all aspects of life.

Fehu

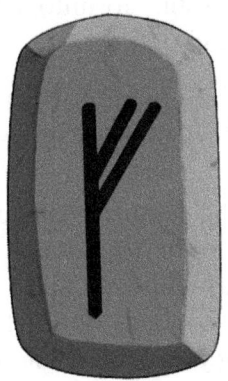

Fehu is a reminder of the present.
https://pixabay.com/images/id-6508602/

Keywords: Prosperity, physical and financial concerns, money, goals, karma, promotion, self-esteem.

Meaning: Fehu is a reminder of our present and the catalyst that awakens a desire to find what lies beyond. It grounds you to your physical location during spiritual journeys and magic acts. It also represents finding what you truly need rather than what you think you desire. Most importantly, Fehu shows that to change your current financial situation, you must first see what changes are possible for you in the future.

Uruz

Keywords: Energy, instinct, vitality, sexuality, wildness, irrationality, fertility, a rite of passage.

Meaning: Uruz represents the acknowledgment of divine forces in nature. Often associated with the god of the sacred hunt, the energy of this rune holds an elemental power that comes from fire. Uruz signals the change from childhood to adulthood and is often used in rituals celebrating this occasion. As the soul within a body matures, it's given a glimpse of the powers of nature.

Thurisaz

Keywords: Hardship, discipline, pain, acknowledgment of inner emotions, awareness of the outside world.

Meaning: Thurisaz depicts an obstacle and foreshadows pain and suffering. However, this suffering is needed to grow and become a stronger version of yourself. What may seem like a huge blow to your ego may be a lesson to push you to make changes happen. Thurisaz tells you that you should allow your destiny to unfold as it should and experience what life has to offer you - good or bad.

Ansuz

Keywords: Leadership, shaman, clairvoyance, the balance of the mind, body, and soul, justice.

Meaning: Representing the ultimate balance, Ansuz signals a point in life where most people choose to remain. When your energies are aligned, you have a sense of fulfillment, and you're tempted to stay in the present. However, Ansuz also points out that you can still make positive changes, further empowering your spiritual and emotional connection with yourself and becoming who you are meant to be.

Raido

Keywords: Change, destiny, journey, fate, progress, progress, life lessons, quest.

Meaning: Raido symbolizes the interwoven twines of fate, representing a web of relationships. Each string is a bond, and every time one crosses another, you gain new connections from the old one. This also means that you can make changes in one relationship without affecting the other ones. Raido shows that you must be aware of all your connections. You can make changes and achieve the desired progress, but your relationships will be affected.

Kenaz

Keywords: Creativity, insight, solution, inspiration, inner wisdom, enlightenment.

Meaning: Kenaz is a rune that brings the obvious solution by giving you subtle messages about the answers you're seeking. While the complete answer may not be revealed to you immediately, this should motivate you to seek the missing parts yourself. Kenaz is the torch that enlightens the path you'll need to follow on your journey and the one that eliminates the darkness surrounding you.

Gebo

Keywords: Gift, generosity, sudden good fortune, relationship, partnership, love, marriage.

Meaning: Often referred to as the rune of connection, Gebo is the first rune that encourages you to break away from the solitary path. It shows you that paying attention to those whose destinies intersect with yours can bring even greater enlightenment. Nurturing your bonds with your loved ones is one of the greatest gifts you can give and receive. It strengthens your relationships and empowers you as a person.

Wunjo

Keywords: Reward, recognition, success, achievement, contentment, fulfillment, joy.

Meaning: As the last rune of the first aett, Wunjo represents the end of a natural cycle and the outset of another. Despite the possibility of a new beginning, you may feel sad that the old has ended, which can leave you stuck in your current position. However, you must realize that your life still holds many lessons, and you must continue your journey. Because the fulfillment you now feel is temporary, and when it passes, you will still feel the need to move on.

Heimdall's Aett

Heimdall is the Norse god of silence and wisdom, known for teaching mankind the universe's rules. He is also said to be a great warrior, often watching out for Loki's malicious tricks and ready to counteract them. The runes of Heimdall's aett warn you about the disruptive forces that cause major shifts in your life. These may change the steady conditions established by the first aett, but you can still make the most of them. The aett helps you navigate the challenging aspects of your life and reminds you that nothing is permanent. The great trials foreshadowed by this aett will forge your character, allowing you to get in touch with your true purpose in life. With their help, you'll learn about the importance of loss and accepting the last phase of a cycle, no matter how painful it may be.

Hagalaz

Keywords: Drastic change, sudden loss, disaster, ordeal, karmic lesson, destruction, clearance, testing.

Meaning: Hagalaz is known to be a harsh wake-up call showing you that you really need to change. Otherwise, you will never achieve happiness.

It's a rather abrupt change after the complacency of the previous rune, especially if you take that for granted. While it's often viewed as a negative sign, it doesn't necessarily have to be. If you choose to embrace the experience instead of refusing to learn your lesson, you can make a difference.

Naudhiz

Keywords: Hardship, poverty, responsibility, obstacle, discontent, frustration.

Meaning: Perhaps to compensate for Hagalaz's hard slap, Naudhiz continues to reinforce the need for change - but more subtly. After communicating with the rune, it often comes as a feeling of discomfort as you realize something isn't as it should be. Naudhiz shows you that if something doesn't go as planned, it means you need to do things differently. Now, you are faced with the dilemma of how to restore the balance between what you want and what you actually *need*.

Isa

Keywords: Stagnation, inactivity, patience, blockage, potential, isolation, reflection.

Meanings: Just as the calm before the storm, Isa represents a period of rest before an abrupt change. It encourages you to take some time to reflect on what you want to achieve and what kind of changes you need. It shows you that although there will always be obstacles, taking the right approach is the key to overcoming them. Isa also allows you to collect your strength so you can face the change when it happens.

Jera

Keywords: Productivity, motion, change, cycle, development, reward.

Meaning: After the period of frozen inactivity granted by Isa comes Jera with the promise of a new beginning. This rune indicates the time for change, growth, and development. You can leave your dissatisfaction behind and enjoy the new flow of positive energy. Your life may not have turned out as planned so far, but this doesn't mean it never will. Jera prompts you to implement your new plans and achieve your dreams.

Eihwaz

Keywords: Initiation, death, change, transformation.

Meanings: Eihwaz marks the turning point in your life's journey by launching you into the transformation phase of the much-needed change. As the symbol of death, Eihway is often viewed as a tool for a passage into maturity and wisdom. Experiencing these changes may be a frightening experience for you, but giving up is not an option. After all, everyone must go through a little suffering before they can reap their spiritual rewards.

Pertho

Keywords: Rebirth, a new beginning, fertility, mystery, divination, sexuality.

Meanings: After accepting the end of a cycle and the abrupt change brought on by the new one, Pertho is there to guide you through the process of rebirth. According to Norse myths, Pertho is the rune that allows you to continue your predestined path through life's perpetual cycles and all the ups and downs. Using this will help you better understand this journey and accept all the changes, whether they are positive or negative.

Algiz

Keywords: Protection, support, assistance, warning, defense.

Meanings: After going through a rebirth, you must face how the changes affect the world around you. Algiz prompts you to use your newfound wisdom wisely to contemplate how your actions reflect on your relationships. It's time to stop focusing on your own spiritual development and see how you can achieve the same. This is another crucial point in life where you must stop and consider your next path.

Sowilu

Keywords: Success, power, positive energy, health, fertility, action.

Meaning: As the last rune in the second aett, Sowilu marks the completion of your individual spiritual journey. Now that you have had time to rest, you'll be ready to launch into action again. The rune encourages you to use the energy you've gathered while resting and move on even if you don't feel the need for it yet. After communicating with this rune, you'll certainly feel the transient nature of your current power.

Tyr's Aett

Tyr is the Norse god of war, also known for his sense of justice and ability to bring order. He is a daring champion who sacrificed his arm to Fenrir so the other deities could trap the giant wolf threatening them all. The runes in Tyr's aett represent a higher spiritual connection, a way to reach the divine forces and seek guidance from them. They allow you to cross that invisible line between the realms and reach out to the divine spirits. At the same time, the runes maintain the connections within human communities, preventing you from losing your sense of humanity. In a way, these rules represent the culmination of all the knowledge acquired from the previous two aettir. They enable you to shift the focus from your individual position and pay attention to the multiple dimensions of your relationships, satisfying nature's laws.

Teiwaz

Keywords: Responsibility, duty, discipline, self-sacrifice, strength, conflict.

Meaning: The first rune of this aett marks a necessary loss brought on by ethical responsibilities. Just as Tyr surrendered his hand in a noble gesture, Teiwaz indicates the sacrifices you'll need to make for the greater good. You can use this rune to tap into the power of its ruling deity and follow up with your duties and responsibilities toward those you encounter on your life's journey.

Berkana

Berkana represents a person who brings positive energy.
https://pixabay.com/images/id-2644529/

Keywords: New beginnings, abundance, fertility, growth, health.

Meaning: Berkana represents the path of a person who brings positive energy into the lives of those around them. Often associated with the birch tree, this symbol is the runic equivalent of spiritual abundance. It helps you heal old wounds and restore frail connections with your loved ones. Berkana also symbolizes fertility in all aspects of life as it fills you with the energy you can use to develop many creative ideas.

Ehwaz

Keywords: Assistance, transportation, energy, motion, hurried decisions, communication.

Meaning: By reminding you that you need to take control, Ehwaz is a rune that promotes balance between all aspects of your life. After gaining all that power, you can't just allow it to roam aimlessly - because if you do, you may end up hurting those around you. To avoid losing the affection of someone, you must listen to the warning of Ehwaz and find the balance and the control you need to navigate your social connections.

Mannaz

Keywords: Family, relationships, community, sense of belonging.

Meaning: Mannaz is the rune that truly puts forward your relationships with your family and friends. It prompts you to form new relationships while nurturing the old ones, satisfying your need for social interaction. However, you must consider how your approach to one relationship affects your other connections. Mannaz will allow you to see all the lives you touch on your journey, teaching you to be more thankful for all the bonds you've formed.

Laguz

Keywords: Fears, negative emotions, secrets, intuition, revelation counseling.

Meaning: Laguz is a rune that'll make you confront your deepest fears regarding your relationships. It encourages you to stop and look at the potential reasons you can't achieve further spiritual development. These reasons are often in our connections with those around us, so by prompting you to help others, this rune can unlock the path toward a higher calling. This will allow you to develop empathy and share your emotions.

Ingwaz

Keywords: Productivity, work, grounding, balance, plenty, nature.

Meaning: For those who long to regain connection with nature, Ingwaz can be a valuable tool. This rune reminds you of our connection with the land, something that's been lost during the industrial revolutions. It can help you find the balance between spirituality and having a productive life without risking getting lost in either of these worlds.

Dagaz

Keywords: Happiness, satisfaction, success, positive activity.

Meanings: Having found the balance between natural life and social interactions, Dagaz will help you reinforce this connection. It acts as a compass, and by following its points, you can find the perfect balance in your life. It reminds you that harmony is possible, which will fill you with a meaningful sense of satisfaction and happiness.

Othila

Keywords: Home, land, property, permanence, belonging, legacy.

Meaning: Othila reminds you that the spiritual wealth you now have access to will surpass the value of the material riches you were promised by Fehu. Whereas physical property was transient, and you were reminded of its possible loss in the second aett, your spiritual legacy will be permanent. This rune marks the end of your journey, where you know who you are destined to be. All the lessons you learned during your travels are now ready to be integrated into your life.

Meditating with the Runes of Each Aett

Like any other form of mindfulness exercise, runic meditation requires physical and mental preparation. Physical preparation means finding a quiet environment where you can focus your mind and won't be disturbed for a couple of minutes. Depending on your practice and preference, it may also involve cleansing your space and body from negative influences.

When it comes to mental preparation, this is usually the first step of the actual meditation, which is done in the following manner:

- Get into a comfortable position. You can sit, stand, or lie down, as long as your back is straight, and you can relax your body.
- Take a few deep breaths to calm your body and stop your racing mind.
- When you feel you can focus on your intention, say a quick prayer to the deity you want to connect with.
- If you are making an offering, too, you can present it right after the prayer.
- Now visualize the rune you want to connect with. If you are addressing more than one, do it slowly and take your time to focus on the image of one before moving on to the next.
- Having formed an image of a rune, exhale deeply and recite the rune name, followed by the phrase representing your intention.
- Inhale again, visualize the next rune, and chant it by drawing it out in your mind and reciting the intention or phrase you want to associate it with.

- If you have trouble focusing on the image of the rune while chanting your intention, feel free to stop reciting and go back to forming the image once again.
- Continue until you've finished with all the runes you want to connect with.
- Return to the present by exhaling slowly and let your mind be filled with thoughts of everyday life.

Ensure the thoughts you address to the runes and the deities ruling the aett they belong to are sincere, positive, and purposeful. You can express your gratitude, seek guidance or peek into the future but only if your intentions have depths to them. You can meditate with more than one rune during one session but keep to the same family. If you seek guidance from more than one deity, you can do it by dedicating a quick session to them on separate days. For example, you can address Frey on Friday, Tyr or Tuesday, Heimdall on Wednesday, etc.

Since the thoughts associated with the runes should be significant for you, it's a good idea to formulate them yourself. Depending on where you currently find yourself in your life's journey and the type of guidance you need, these thoughts can address immediate issues or even long-term goals. Here are a few examples of what you can say when focusing on a run:

- **Fehu:** I know that wealth is power, and I will ward my wealth.
- **Thurisaz:** If I develop my own strength, I know that my power will never fail me.
- **Hagalaz:** The hail of Heimdall is pure, and it will wash away anything bad, revealing the good.
- **Jera:** My achievements will be proportionate to my efforts. The more work I put in, the more rewards I will reap.
- **Tiwaz:** To be happy and successful, I must adhere to order and discipline.
- **Ingwaz:** The key to success is to plan and withhold my power so I can release it at the best possible time.

Chapter 5: The Magic of the Runes and Staves

Historically, runes were used both for writing and for magic. There appears to be a specific power associated with each rune. When combined into magical staves or used alongside spells, runes were used as tools for specific magical purposes, including spiritual transformation and personal growth.

But what is it about the Elder Futhark runes that make them have this kind of mystical power?

Next, we will explore the history of the runes and why they are associated with magic. You will then learn about the magical properties of each rune and how they can be combined to create your own spells and charms.

A Brief Source History of Magical Runes

Runic inscriptions can be found throughout history. There is no defined linear narrative of runes as magical items. Rather, the evidence is scattered along an undefined timeline. This narrative contains inscriptions of historical references, literature, and mysterious carvings such as magical charms and phrases.

Historic Literature about Magical Runes

The Poetic Edda is an untitled collection of Old Norse narrative poetry found in the Codex Regius written during the late 1200s. It contains numerous sources of runic magic. One of the best sources is the Sigrdrífumál, a poem that contains verses detailing how a Valkyrie blessed a hero with the knowledge of runes. Among the other works in this collection, there are poems and stanzas about runes that tell how they are used in spells being taught among the characters mentioned. There is talk of casting a charm spell with the "gladness rune" and other rune names. In all instances, the runes are used for actual magic and ability-enhancing spells.

Besides literature, the runes also appear in numerous Norse myths. Among them, the Norse myth of Odin and the World Tree is credited with inspiring Elder Futhark's runic system. A description of this can be found in the Poetic Edda's Havamàl. The tale of Odin and Loki creating a magical spear with the help of runes so it would never miss its target is one of the most famous tales.

Historical Evidence of Magical Runes

Protective inscriptions and "alu" rune words were discovered during the Roman and Germanic Iron Ages. Carved into spears, shafts, and even bone, these inscriptions appear to have been proliferated by an Erilaz, translated into "runemaster" or "magician."

It has also been documented that charms and spells were made using runes as early as 98AD. Roman politician and historian Publius Cornelius Tacitus, widely regarded as one of the greatest Roman historians by modern scholars, described magical methods and their strict adherence. He mentioned what appears to be spell casting using signs together with natural objects like tree bark and white cloth. He then described the careful inspection and reverence of these signs. This practice appears to be widespread among the community, with family and the state priest in attendance. While the term "signs" is often disputed, it is generally accepted that this refers to written documentation of magical runes in practice.

Historical Evidence of the Magical Purpose of Runes

The Kingmoor Ring, among others, bears runic inscriptions of apparent magical significance. And two runestones in Sweden contain the phrase "runes of power" inscribed upon them.

The Glavendrup stone is a runestone found in Denmark and dates from the early 10th century. It contains a warning curse inscription carved on the stone.

What Makes Runes Magical?

Now that we know some of the historical references to the runes' magical properties, let's look at *how* they were used.

Having discussed the history of the runes in previous chapters, we know they form the Elder Futhark alphabet, a sequence of 24 letters meaning "secret" or "mystery" in the Gothic language. The Germanic peoples of Northern Europe used them for divination, magic, and as powerful talismans and protective amulets in ancient times.

The Norse and other Northern European people didn't use the rune letters for communication and trade. Instead, they marked graves, honored ancestors, and predicted the future with them. They represented great mysteries, morality, and divination. Runes stones were thought to emanate powerful magical properties and were highly venerated due to their historical narrative and so were taken very seriously.

Besides serving as a symbol of cosmic conditions and reverence for higher powers, the runes also served a ritual purpose. The runes influenced every aspect of life, from the sacred to the practical. Health and love were controlled by spells and runes, as were crops, the sea, and the weather. There were runes for death and birth, fertility, and spells to end curses. They decorated houses for safe keeping and Viking ships for protection and strength. Runes were also carved on weapons, food platters, and jewelry.

Elder Futhark Runes- Magical Meaning

Below is a quick reference list of magical and divinatory meanings. This list is not exhaustive, and some meanings overlap.

Rune	Magical Uses
OTHALA / O	Influence over possessions, inheritance, experience, ancestry, heritage, and value.
LAGUZ / L	Stabilize emotions and turmoil, enhance psychic abilities, uncover the truth, and confront fears.

Rune	Name	Meaning
ᛖ	EHWAZ / E	Energy, power, trust, progress, communication, progress, change, transportation.
ᛏ	TIWAZ / T	Victory, protection, reinforce will, strength, healing a wound, analysis.
ᛉ	ALGIZ / Z	Channeling energy, a shield, Protection, ward against evil, guardian.
ᛇ	EIHWAZ / E / I	To ease a life transition, defense, transformation, protection, cause change.
ᛁ	ISA / I	Reinforcement of other magics, ice, obstacles, blockages, freezing, and reflection.
ᚺ	HAGALAZ / H	Destructive, dangerous weather, breaking destructive patterns, the wrath of nature, uncontrolled forces.
ᚷ	GEBO / G	Balance, luck, fertility, successful partnering, giving.
ᚱ	RAIDHO / R	Bring about change, protection for travelers, rhythm, facilitate change, and reconnection.
ᚦ	THURISAZ / TH	Focus on getting rid of the negative, regeneration, concentration, and self-discipline.

Rune	Name	Meaning
ᚠ	FEHU / F	Achieve goals, luck, new beginnings, abundance, success, luck.
ᛞ	DAGAZ / D	Clarity, positivity, awakening, awareness, transformation.
ᛝ	INGWAZ / NG	Strength, growth, health, balance, grounded, connect.
ᛗ	MANNAZ / M	Order in life, intelligence, thought, ability, skill, create.
ᛒ	BERKANA / B	Start again, encouragement, desire, healing, regeneration, liberation.
ᛋ	SOWILO / S	Cosmic force, energy, healing, strength, cleansing, success.
ᛈ	PERTHRO / P	Knowledge of secrets, fertility, enhance the self and powers, control uncertainty.
ᛃ	JERA / J/ Y	Fruition, eliminate stagnation, growth, harvest, create change.
ᚾ	NAUTHIZ / N	Survival, frustration, endurance, obstacles, determination.

Rune	Meaning
ᚹ WUNJO / W	Happiness, harmony, joy, prosperity, success, motivation.
ᚲ KENAZ / C/ K	Light, motivation, regeneration, inspiration, regeneration.
ᚨ ANSUZ / A	Leadership, communication, wisdom, signals, health.
ᚢ URUZ / U	Understanding, strength, speed, energy, courage, dedication, vitality.

No matter the level of knowledge you have of the Elder Futhark alphabet or where you are at in your learning process, having a guide with each rune name and magical meaning is always helpful.

How Are Runes Used in Spells?

Technically speaking, there is no way to know how our ancestors cast spells with runes. There is, however, some evidence of spell casting through speech, singing, and writing.

There are generally two ways to cast spells with runes. Either write it down and place it with the runes on a cloth, mat, or bowl- known as a talisman. The talisman then transmits its power to your writing. Or cast the spell through speech or chant- known as incantations. In his book "Futhark: A Handbook of Rune Magic," Edred Thorsson devised a specific chant for each rune to create a mantra. But you can do it any way you want.

How Can Runes Be Used to Perform Magic?

Runes could also be used to perform divination. They help manifest intent into physical manifestation by interacting with internal and external energies.

When placing your runes on your item and writing or carving them, a fluid is placed over them. The most common bodily fluids are blood or spit. The runes are typically stained red by alcohol or red dye (blood symbolism). Then, either the rune's name or a short incantation of your choice may be used. A spell may need to be carried or placed near the target of the spell, depending on where it will exert its influence.

Combine Runes to Make Powerful Charms

Between the 15th and 19th centuries, magical charms/staves were found according to Icelandic literature. Staves are made when you combine rune symbols to create an even more powerful magical effect. They were carved into stone, wood, or paper and carried around or placed in the homestead or on ships for protection. An individual's connection with the rune is strengthened when runes are carved manually.

Vikings believed that, when correctly used, runes could manifest ideas.

Vegvísir Viking Stave

Among the most popular staves is the Viking Vegvísir. A magic stave is meant to guide its bearer through rough weather. A map depicting a Vegvísir, which means "that which shows the way," was compiled by Geir Vigfusson in the 19th century. Instead of the round symbol used today, the Huld Manuscript uses a square symbol with eight staves, each ending with a different symbol. Some speculate that each rune symbol represented a direction point, similar to a compass.

The Helm of Awe Stave

The Helm of Awe stave is one of the most recognizable Icelandic symbols, and it is said to provide protection and strength in the battle for anyone wearing it.

There is a strong connection between the Helm of Awe and the runes because some of the shapes on the stave are similar to runes. It is highly unlikely that this correspondence was just a coincidence, given how central the runes were to Germanic magic. The stave used various rune symbols, including the Algiz (Z) rune. Considering this is a rune for strength and protection, it makes sense that it would be used in their stave. It also uses the Isa (I) rune meaning blockage of obstacles.

Rune Spells

Not only was it possible to use runes for divination, but it was also used to obtain desired results. In times of desire, people drew or carved on wood and stone corresponding to runic characters and kept them with them at all times as a reminder of their wishes and desires. Wishes that came true due to runic spells would be burned in open flames once the scripts had worked.

It can be a bit confusing when you're just starting out with Rune Magic to figure out how to perform spells. Here is a simple, step-by-step beginner spell.

How to Make a Spell with Runes

Studying the runes and understanding their meanings first is the most critical step in this process. The final spell could have a different outcome that might affect its general purpose, so you must be careful about what runes you mix together.

Consequently, don't let this prospect put you off. Practicing as much as possible is the best way to learn! Take a look at some of the spells others are doing, and analyze them until you become more knowledgeable on spell making.

1. This is about what you want to achieve with this spell. Use the above chart that describes each rune and its magical properties.
2. After you have looked at the runes, take some time to visualize what you want from this spell. Do you want to be happy and prosper? Imagine yourself in a serene meadow of golden sunflowers.
3. To really make your spell power, you should carefully consider the runes. Think about the meaning and symbolism behind each of the runes. You may find that one or two pop out at you without warning - as if they're waiting for you.
4. To start, only pick 2 runes. You don't want to overcomplicate things when you're just starting out. Take things slowly until you get the hang of it. It is also a good idea to take special care when combining the runes. Working with runes isn't as simple as it seems, and some of them have different meanings than you may think. Make sure you do a lot of research into the history of each

rune to select the right one for your purpose.

5. Creating your design is now the next step. We are looking at binding the runes for this spell to create an extra powerful effect. You'll need some paper and a pen. Don't overthink this step. Let your thoughts loose and just go with the flow. The less time you spend thinking about it, the more your inner desire will emerge. Start drawing as much fusing of the symbols as you wish. Feel free to let your imagination run wild and draw whatever comes to mind.
6. Let the drawing settle for a few minutes once you've completed it.
7. Now, take a look at your drawings and choose the one that speaks to you – whichever seems to pop out of the page.
8. Next, pick any material to bind the runes together. If you're casting a self-purpose spell, you will have to carry it around with you. So, choose something practical like stone, fabric, or wood – or turn it into a decoration, frame it, and hang it on your bedroom wall. If the spell is only for a short time, then a piece of paper will usually do the trick.
9. Now, it's time to create the ritual. You know what you want to create your spell, you have chosen the runes to enact it, plus you have your materials ready and waiting. Now, charge your charm with energy and power.
10. Do this next step in any way you want. Some people like to light candles and go into a meditative trance or somewhere quiet away from the outside world. As you draw or carve your rune, it is vital that you keep your purpose in mind.
11. The most important thing is to remain present and in the moment, without losing track of the task at hand, and carve out each of the runes of the bind rune one by one until you have completed the final design of the rune. Take a moment to think about what the meaning of each rune is and how it will help you.
12. Some people like to take a moment afterward to really soak up the event. Again, always remain aware of the purpose of your spell and what you want to achieve from it. Manifestation of desires is one of the main concepts of the runes, after all. Make sure you stay in your thoughts while holding the charm tightly in your hands.

Well done! You have now created your very first rune bind, and it's time to use it. It's not as difficult as you may think to recall the magic of runes. All you have to do to ensure it works is to keep it on or around you until it does its job. Keep it in your bag when you go to work. In addition, if you use more than one bag, for example, at the gym, make sure you swap the charm into the other bag. Put it somewhere you won't forget about it, like in your bedroom.

To maintain the spell's intention, keep it with you at all times.

You can dispose of your bind rune as soon as you achieve your goal. Naturally, this depends on the binding source you used during the spell. If you used wood or stone, it's perfectly fine for you to bury it. A charm can be buried in a place that holds special meaning for some people. If you use paper, you can simply burn it by dropping it into an open flame or lighting it with a candle.

Originally, runes were designed to be used as letters in a language. However, they were much more than letters. By writing or engraving a runic symbol, one invoked and directed the force represented by it. The runes symbolize a meaningful exchange between us and the invisible world. They represent a powerful history that brings people together with nature and the universe.

Chapter 6: Creating and Activating Your Runes

We've already explained the history of the magical properties of the Elder Futhark runes and how they were used as an ancient form of prophecy by those seeking advice.

Now, we will discuss the activation methods in relation to your charm through charging and meditative techniques. If you want your runes to speak to you, they need to be activated. We will then go on to how you can create your very own divination set and how to activate it.

The rune needs to be activated to work.
https://unsplash.com/photos/cBkHr5RuooA

Activating Your Rune Charm

If you followed the guide to making your own rune charm in chapter 5, we will now go a little deeper into how to *activate it*. Knowing how to activate your rune for various purposes is a great skill to have. It is also fun to learn all the different techniques you will be able to add to your divination arsenal.

We will provide you with two activation techniques. The first will rely on a meditative technique using the power of the North Star, also known as Odin's Eye. The other activation technique will involve the properties of Galdr and the ancient form of magical chanting.

Odin's Eye Activation

Sprinkle salt on your charm before charging it and leave it overnight. Salt acts as a cleansing tool, and it also offers protective powers.

Tools:

- Rune charm
- Smoke from herbs/candles
- Compass
- White cloth
- Quiet room
- Table
- Incense

Instructions:

1. Find a quiet spot in your home.
2. Cover the table with your cloth
3. In the center of the table, place the herbs or candle and the incense.
4. Place your charm next to them.
5. Imagine that your charm is the essence of life and that its essence is meant to create a richer, more fulfilling life for you. Then spend a few minutes reflecting on the meaning of your charm.
6. Using the compass, locate North and position yourself and the table facing it.

7. Keeping your eyes closed, place the charm into the palm of your hands, or hover your hand palms over the charm.
8. Put yourself in a meditative state and imagine that the brightness of the Northern Star is pulling you as you meditate. As you get closer, and the light gets brighter, return with the light back through the night sky and into your room. Feel the power of the star flowing through you as you center its energy into your body and mind.
9. Hold the charm up toward the North, thinking deeply about the intention of the charm. Imagine the energy of Odin and the star's energy settling into the charm.

Your charm is now activated.

Galdr Activation

Take note of the names of the runes you used in your charm. We will take the first two or three letters on the runes and combine them to make your Galdr chant. For example, if you used the Ansuz (A) and Dagaz (D) charm to bind the two magical elements together, then your chant could be "An-Dag," "Dag-An," Ans- Da," Da- Ans," "Ans-Dag," or "Dag-Ans." Whichever combination you choose will be just as effective as any other.

Then, when you want to activate your rune charm, you can sit and chant this Galdr while using it in your ritual.

What Can Runes Be Used For?

Did you know that runes can be used for other things besides creating charms and casting spells? They can be used in the art of divination too. First, ask yourself why you want to create your own rune set in the first place. Runes can provide guidance and insight into how things may turn out. They don't act as a fortune-telling tool per se, nor can they offer you solid advice or answers. They can offer insight into your unique situation, which can, in turn, provide you with correct reactionary awareness.

Runic readers recognize that the future isn't predetermined and that individuals can make their own choices. Because of this, you are more than welcome to change the direction if you don't like what you get from a rune reading.

There are many situations where runes can be used. Consulting the runes can be helpful when you have limited information or cannot see the whole picture.

How Does Rune Divination Work?

Remember when you were introduced to casting your first spell in chapter 5? Throughout the process, we stressed the importance of keeping your objective in mind. This is because runes focus on your conscious and subconscious mind when you ask a question or think about an issue. A rune is not entirely random when it is cast in front of you but rather a choice made by your subconscious.

It is common to use runes for divination. Most modern-day users will utilize them to seek answers or even achieve success. In most respects, contemporary runes differ from Elder Futhark runes in that they are far more related to 21st-century questions like inner peace and prayer. You will still be able to interpret your runes easily even though they will possess the same qualities as those used in ancient times.

What Sort of Runes Do I Need for Divination?

Various materials can be used to make runes, including stone, wood, clay, metal, pebbles, bones, and crystals. If you're just starting out and you're trying to find out if you enjoy rune casting, then a simple rune set will be more than enough.

However, once you've practiced for a while and have developed a passion for runes, you'll probably want to have a *divination set* made up of quartz or crystals. These types of sets can be purchased and will usually come with an instruction leaflet on how to use and interpret them.

But, if the runes' history and origin resonated with you, you will probably understand the importance of making your own runes and divination set. Not only does this help you more to understand the concept of runes, but it will bring you closer to them. If they're carved with care and attention, they will be formed as a part of you. Therefore, they will be more likely to understand your energy and provide a more personal insight into your questions and problems. No matter what the material is, it's the way you use the runes that matters most, not what the runes look like.

Rune Divination Set

Just a quick note about the number of runes you need to create. A runic alphabet consists of 24 letters, and the Elder Futhark is the most common for rune divination. This is the set you will be using as inspiration when making yours. Some rune sets include a blank rune, referred to as Odin's rune or Wyrd rune. Some people accept this blank rune as the unknown aspect of fate, while others believe there is no historical evidence that this rune ever existed when the Elder Futhark letters were created. Nonetheless, it is up to you if you want to include it in your divination set. If you do, you will create 25 runes instead of just 24. However, if this is your first time making a set, you may want to make more and err on the side of caution. This way, if you make a mistake during the carving process, you can pick a spare rune without making another one.

It is essential to keep your divination set simple when making your first one. Start by thinking of health, success, strength, and other intents you would frequently use with your runes. You will become more familiar with your runes and will be more sincere about their creation as you spend more time crafting them. Since you've spent a lot of time creating them, charging them will be easier when the time comes. Make each one as significant as the last. We will get into charging them later on.

How to Create Your Own Rune Divination Set

The most common traditional materials for runes were stone or wood. This was because they were simple enough to carve lines into. These days though, we have much better access to molding materials. So, for this divination set, we will use polymer sculpting clay that hardens in the oven because it is easy to find and use. Plus, it is non-toxic and won't make a mess while you're using it.

Tools:
- Polymer clay
- Spatula
- Pencil
- Small carving tool
- Oven set to 110 degrees Celsius/230 degrees Fahrenheit
- Foil or baking sheet
- Black acrylic paint
- Thin paint brush
- A damp cloth or wet wipe
- Clear casting resin

Instructions:
1. Roll some small balls of clay in between your hands (24 for the Elder Futhark alphabet, 25 if you want to include the blank rune.

Or more if you want to have spares just in case you make any mistakes during carving).

2. Flatten them out using a spatula to avoid fingerprints. Not too thick, around 0.5 cm / 0.19 inches.
3. You can make them into any size you want- big or small, it's up to you. This is an advantage of making your own.
4. This next step is optional, but we will make the runes into charms for duality too. So, take a pencil or something sharp with a tip, and poke a hole through the top of each piece of flattened clay. This way, you can use the runes as charms and wear them as a necklace.
5. Now, we will carve the rune letters into the clay pieces. You can use a pencil or a small clay spatula.
6. Carve each symbol into the rune about 1- 2 mm in depth. This way, the symbols will be clear when baked.
7. Take your time when carving the symbols, and remember if you want to use them as charms, then keep the hole for the charm at the top.
8. After you have finished carving, place your clay pieces onto a foil or baking sheet and onto a baking tray.
9. Place them into the oven at around 110 degrees Celsius / 230 degrees Fahrenheit and bake them for around 30 minutes.
10. After 30 minutes, the clay pieces will be hardened. Leave them to cool for another 30 minutes.
11. This next step is optional, but it does help to make the symbols stand out more. Take your black acrylic paint and brush and carefully paint into the indents of the rune carvings.
12. After painting each rune symbol, things may look a little messy. If so, take a damp cloth and carefully wipe away any residue. This step won't rub the paint away as the carvings will be deep enough to hold the paint inside rather than outside.
13. Leave the paint to dry.
14. To keep your runes from wear and tear (and looking nice and sturdy), paint the runes with a clear resin. This will give them a nice shine. Again, leave the resin to dry.

And there you have it. Your very own divination set is carved and created with care and attention.

Activating Your Divination Set

When we say activating, we mean charging the set with energy. This doesn't necessarily mean charging them with the power of a full moon but instead igniting them with your spirit and trust.

Runes are a tool for divination, but their interpretation relies on the human essence within each individual. Therefore, every divination practice begins with some form of ritual designed to quieten the mind and reconnect the reader with their intuition.

The next step is to put your question out into the universe, again using your mind's power. The Vikings believed that all natural forces in the world were interconnected. In other words, if you ask a question with intent, the historical forces that were so revered by the ancient use of runes can help you find an answer.

For the activation to be a success, there is, however, one thing to note before you start. During activation, you must know the meaning of each of the runes. This will ensure you initiate the correct essence of the rune meaning.

Some people choose to use tag locks in this part of the activation ritual. This means the use of bodily fluids like blood or spit. But if you're not comfortable with using bodily fluids, you can still activate the runes with the same connection by following these steps.

1. For those interested in using a tag lock with their runes, you need to dab each of the runes with a little of your blood or saliva as you follow the steps below. If you're not interested in locking any bodily fluids into the runes (it's not absolutely necessary, and we don't want you to hurt yourself!), then by all means, skip this step.
2. Take each of your runes, one by one, and either place it against your forehead, over your heart, or hold it between the palms of your hands.
3. Actively visualize it in your mind as you do this. Try getting into a meditative stance or prayer if possible.
4. When you feel you're ready, go ahead and dab a little bit of your blood or saliva onto the carving of the rune. As you're doing this, keep saying or chanting the name of the rune.

Runecasters use this step as a way to create a link and hear the rune speak to them, not necessarily with words, as it is more of a feeling.

5. Again, hold the rune against your forehead, heart, or in between the palms of your hands and give it just a moment to charge.

During this step, some prefer to say a specific chant, breathe onto the rune, or say "so mote it be" or "thank you." This can create a bond between you and each of the runes. Remember, there are 24 runes to a set, so you will have to do this activation step at least 24 times. For those who dabbed their runes with fluids, you can add a sealant over them to keep them from chipping away.

Once you have activated the runes and this step is complete, you can cast the runes. They can be thrown down, drawn from a bag, or used in any other way. A rune's position in relation to each other and where it falls will determine how the answer is interpreted.

We will discuss exactly how to read the runes you cast in another chapter. But for now, know that researchers and mystics have developed several different ways to read the runes for divination, and there is a wide range of approaches. Nonetheless, you will discover that every practice relies on connecting with your intuition through the runes.

Taking Care of Your Runes

Cleansing and activating your runes is an integral part of caring for them. Providing you treat runes with respect, they can become a powerful supportive tool. How often you perform your cleansing rituals will depend on a few factors, but essentially it is up to you how often you recharge them. If the runes are new or have been touched by other people, then it makes sense to reactivate their power for them to bind to you and only you. Runes should be kept as close to you as possible since they are often considered personal items. Tuning into your own energy by keeping them close to you at work or in your bedroom will help you receive a more accurate reading.

You can keep your runes in a pouch to keep them safe.
https://unsplash.com/photos/vzrKcFry8Sc

Runes can be stored in a box, or a bag made of natural materials. In addition to velvet pouches, some prefer wooden boxes with a selenite stick inside. Selenite is a natural healing crystal, so its properties can emit powerful healing energy to your runes.

You should always remain emotionally centered no matter how you activate your rune charms or divination set. It is possible for the higher forces that you call upon to have either a positive or negative reaction to your questions, depending on your inner feelings during the ritual.

By now, you should have a better understanding of what it takes to call on the magic of the Elder Futhark runes. Once you are familiar with their meaning, the next step will be for you to activate your rune charms. Once you have done that, the process should energize your creative subconscious into making your own divination set.

Chapter 7: Seiðr: The Art of Runic Divination

In this chapter, you'll learn to develop the ability of Seiðr - the practice of predicting the unknown by reading the Elder Futhark runes. To start with, you'll be given a comprehensive insight into divination in general and Seiðr as a practice and the results you can expect from it. Like any other divination practice, Seiðr requires you to prepare your space, some tools, your body, and your mind. Having gone through these elements, you'll be ready to move on to the topic of rune casting and learn how to use runic spreads as a form of guidance to address current problems or situations. You'll also be provided with a quick recap of the meaning of each runic symbol to help you read them and find the answers you seek.

Divination and Seiðr Basics

Divination is a method of tapping into your intuition to access knowledge hidden from your conscious thought processes. Your subconscious mind communicates what it sees and interprets as spiritual messages, allowing your conscious mind to decipher them. Several forms of divination include dream interpretation, scrying with crystals, using Tarot cards, coins, and tea leaves, and casting runes. Divination through runes is very similar to reading Tarot cards in that it won't help you predict the future. It's a guidance tool that works with your subconscious to solve problems or overcome situations by looking at potential outcomes.

Seiðr is a type of Norse magic related to telling and shaping the future. According to Norse myths, Seiðr was primarily associated with the deities Odin and Freya, who then taught the practice to the other Norse Deities. Later, the practice was passed on to mankind in general and was said to be reserved for the females of each generation. Nowadays, practitioners of Norse Magic still use Seiðr as a reliable divinatory practice.

To perform Seiðr, a practitioner must enter a trance to interact with the divine forces. Then, they ask questions related to prophesy or guidance for future actions. The Seiðr rituals may be performed to seek out hidden knowledge - whether it's hidden in a physical location or in your mind, attracting good luck and many other attainable purposes. In ancient times, they were also done to heal the sick, control the weather, settle disputes, and bring the opposite of all the above. However, since the method revolves around questions from the past, present, and future, casting and consistently interpreting runes is nearly impossible. The only way to practice Seiðr divination reliably is to use it for attainable, conscious goals.

What You Need for Practicing Divination

The first thing you'll need to practice runic divination is a set of runes. Here, you can either buy a set of pre-made runes or make your own, as many practitioners of Norse Paganism do. While the first is probably easier for newbies, making runes enhances your connection with them, which makes them work even better for you. If you go for the first option, you can choose between runes made from stone, wood, and crystals. Carving runes into crystals infuses them with an added element called natural vibrations, which can be used for various purposes.

If you choose to create your own runes, you can inscribe them into pieces of stones or nut-bearing wood, like hazel, oat, pine, or even cedar. Apart from carving, you can also paint the symbols with acrylic paint (highly recommended for beginners) or burn them into the wood (only recommended if you have experience using burning tools). Carving your own runes can be part of the magical preparation process for any spell, divination, or other magical act. It can be beneficial for your practice, but it shouldn't be taken lightly; otherwise, you'll miss out on infusing your runes with your powers.

You'll also need to prepare a surface to work on. This can be your altar or any other sacred space you usually practice in. If you are going for the cloth method, you will need to lay a piece of fabric on your prepared surface. You may use any type of incense, candles, oils, crystals, or any other tools that help you get into the right frame of mind to access the information you seek. Apart from these items and the runes, you may prepare symbols of the guide you are working with. If you are seeking divinatory guidance from a Norse deity, you should have something that symbolizes them. This can be a picture, an object, or the drawing of the rune that represents them.

Runecasting

Runecasting is a popular oracular divination method used by practitioners of Norse magic. It involves casting runes to receive guidance to handle problems or situations that you need help with. Runecasting is essentially very similar to Tarot spreads or pulls, as it also offers a better perspective for a variety of situations - some general, others more specific. The latter is a more common purpose, as you have better chances of receiving an answer to a concrete question rather than a generic one.

Each rune of the Elder Futhark has a corresponding meaning, and the ones laid out in front of you will guide you toward possible answers or solutions. That said, just like with any divination method, runes won't give you the exact answer to your questions, nor do they offer direct advice on what you should or shouldn't do with your life. Instead, they suggest different outcomes and factors that may influence these. Runecasting can be a great tool to enhance your intuition and learn to rely on it by applying some critical thinking skills. Like with Tarot spreads, the rules don't reveal anything fixed. Your actions can influence the outcome of different situations and drastically alter them. So, if you don't like an outcome, change what you are currently doing, and the results will be more to your liking.

How to Cast Runes

According to Norse traditions, the runes are cast on white cloth. This provides a neutral background so the caster can focus on the results. The color white is also considered magical and is believed to enhance the forming of the magical bond between the runes and the person casting them. While there are practitioners who prefer casting onto the ground for better access to natural magic, the choice will be up to you.

Some runecasting methods involve tossing the runes in front of you - others will require you to lay them out in an elaborate pattern. With the first ones, you can also choose between keeping your eyes closed or open while looking at the sky during casting. When the runes land, you can open your eyes/lower your head and read them. Casting a runic spread is similar to laying out a Tarot spread. You hold the bag or box in your hand, formulate your questions, and start pulling out the runes one by one. You place them in the shape of the spread you've chosen to interpret.

Whichever method you choose, keep your runes in a bag or box until you are ready to cast them to prevent them from getting infused with negative influences. Before you start the divination process, prepare your space by cleansing it, and you can do the same with your mind and body too. Make sure you have the right questions and intentions in mind by considering your current situation and what you want to achieve in the future. You may even do a meditation exercise preparing your mind to focus or say a quick prayer to the deity you are asking for assistance.

How to Use Runic Divination Spreads

There are a few different layouts that can help you tap into your intuition and reveal the answers to the questions you ask during your divinatory practice. The simplest one is the 1-rune pull, although this isn't truly adequate for divination because it only answers yes or no questions. That said, it can still be great for practice and learning the meanings of the runes, especially if you are familiar with the Tarot, as this is very similar to the daily 1-card reading method. It involves pulling one rune out of your bag and looking at it to interpret its meaning.

You'll need more runes to get information about past and present influences and future outcomes. Popular spreads involving multiple runes are the 3-rune layout, the 5-rune layout, the 7-rune layout, the 9-rune layout, and the 24-rune layout. Before you cast any of the spreads, you should put your hand in the bag you keep your runes in. Move your hands around to shuffle the runes before spreading them. Since runecasting typically addresses a particular issue, you should consider which problem you want to explore. This will help you access the influences of the past and present.

The 3-Rune Layout

This is one of the most ancient layouts, as traditionally, the Norse cast their runes in 3, or multiples of 3. It reveals past, present, and future influences related to simple questions and is often recommended for beginner practitioners.

Here is how to cast it:
- Pull 3 runes out of your bag one at a time, and put them onto the cloth. Make sure you place them side by side with their symbols facing you.
- The first rune indicates your issue in general, so make sure you take a good look at it.
- The second rune shows all the challenges you face as a result of the issue.
- The last rune highlights potential steps you can take to overcome the challenges.

The 5-Rune Layout

Once you get the hang of the 3-rune spread, you can try your hand at the 5-rune layout. The 2 additional runes will help you to explore your issue in detail so you can better understand how your future will be influenced by your past and present.

Here is how to do the 5-rune spread:
- Lay out your runes in the shape of a cross. The bottom rune will represent the fundamental influences over the answers you seek.
- The rune on the far left conveys the problems that lead to the questions.
- The rune on the far right represents the answers to your questions.
- The rune on the top indicates positive influences over the question and answers.
- The last rune, the one in the middle, indicates any possible future influences over the answer.

The 7-Rune Layout

The 7-rune layout reveals past, present, and future influences related to your questions, along with other possible issues you weren't aware of - some of which you may want to explore further.

Here is how to use the 7-rune spread:
- With the runes in your hand, formulate a question (or more).
- Lay out your runes in a V shape and start interpreting the answers and the possible influences over them.

- The first rune in the top left position indicates influences from the past.
- The second rune under it represents the current influences related to the answers.
- The one that follows below shows how future actions may influence the outcome and the truthfulness of the answers.
- The central rune at the bottom of the V indicates possible paths you can take to reach the desired outcome.
- The first rune on the right side above the center highlights any emotions that may influence the questions.
- The rune above it indicates any problems that lead to the question which may influence the outcome.
- Finally, the rune on the top right represents the possible future outcomes of the situation or question you want to learn about.

The 9-Rune Layout

9 is considered a mystical number in Norse mythology, and using them in a rune layout can improve your divination practice. It's also incredibly easy to use, even though it requires 9 different symbols to interpret. Here is how to do it:

- Close your eyes, and scatter 9 runes on a cloth.
- Open your eyes and look at how they landed while paying attention to two factors.
- Are the runes turned over or facing upward? Runes that land on the right side uphold the answer to your questions, while the ones facing down indicate issues related to the questions you aren't aware of yet.
- You should also look at whether the runes have landed closer to the center of the cloth or further away. The former shows the crucial matters you should be concerned about in the future, whereas the latter group pertains to less significant matters.

The 24-Rune Layout

A 24-rune layout is recommended for the beginning of a cycle to reveal what the year may bring you. Apart from the Roman calendar, New Year's Day, the beginning of one's birth year, and the winter solstice also count as the beginning of a new cycle. It's an advanced method as it uses all the 24 runes of the Elder Futhark.

Here is how to do the 24-runic layout spread:

- After formulating your questions, lay out your spread in a 3x8 grid. You will read and interpret each row from right to left.
- The first rune of the first row represents the ways you can obtain financial gain and prosperity.
- The second rune shows the ways you can improve your physical health and strength.
- The third rune shows how you can defend yourself and win over the competition.
- The fourth rune indicates how you can gain wisdom and inspiration for making changes.
- The fifth rune shows you the direction your life path will take during the year.
- The sixth rune reveals all the wisdom you may learn in the upcoming year.
- The seventh rune shows all the skills you can master and hone and the gifts you'll be given.
- The eight runes of the first row represent all the ways you can achieve balance and happiness.
- The first rune of the second row represents the future changes you can expect in your life.
- The second rune indicates what you need to do to achieve your dreams and obtain your goals.
- The third rune represents any obstacles life may throw in your way on your journey.
- The fourth rune highlights your achievements and successes throughout the year.
- The fifth rune indicates any challenges you'll need to conquer and the choices you'll need to make.
- The sixth rune represents all your inner strength and skills that'll manifest.
- The seventh rune represents the most critical situation you'll face during the year.

- The eighth rune will act as a guide for your energy on your journey.
- The first rune of the third row represents any business and legal matters you're a part of.
- The second rune shows how you'll achieve personal growth.
- The third rune indicates all the relationships you'll make and juggle in the upcoming year.
- The fourth rune represents your expected social status.
- The fifth rune shows you how your emotional status may change.
- The sixth rune highlights any romantic situation you'll be part of.
- The seventh rune shows you the ways you will obtain harmony in your life.
- The eighth rune represents all the assets you'll gain throughout the year.

How to Read Each Rune

Once you have your runes spread in front of you, you'll be able to interpret their meanings. The table below shows a quick recap of the primary meaning of each runic symbol.

Freyr's Aett		Heimdall's Aett		Tyr's Aett	
Fehu ᚠ	Cattle/ Wealth	Hagalaz H	Hail	Tiwaz ↑	Victory
Uruz ᚢ	Ox	Nautiz +	Needs	Berkana ᛒ	Birch
Thurisaz ᚦ	Giant/ Thorn	Isa I	Ice	Ehwaz M	Horse
Ansuz ᚠ	Message	Jera ᛋ	Harvest	Mannaz ᛗ	Man
Raido R	Journey	Eihwaz ᛋ	Yew	Laguz ᛚ	Lake

Freyr's Aett		Heimdall's Aett		Tyr's Aett	
Kenaz ‹	Torch	Pertrho ⌊	Destiny	Ingwaz ᛜ	Fertility
Gebo X	Gift	Algiz Y	Elk	Dagaz ᛞ	Dawn
Wunjo ᚹ	Joy	Sowilo ᛇ	Sun	Othila ᛟ	Heritage

However, as you've learned from the previous chapters, each rune of the Elder Futhark has several symbolic associations. For example, Ehwaz means horse, but it's also believed to mean luck or wheel. To get the answers you seek, it's crucial to not only focus on the primary meanings. Instead, you should think about each rune meaning how they relate to your questions. If we follow the example of Ehwaz, you should consider whether your question was about luck, possible travel, sports involving wheels, or horses in general. Think about your situation as well - the questions you ask may not convey what you really want to achieve because you aren't aware of it consciously. For example, if you are down on your luck and Ehwaz comes up in the primary answer position, you should look at the other runes for answers on how you may change your luck. Don't disregard your gut feelings because these are often the key to unlocking the unconscious answers your conscious mind can't process. For example, if you see Ehwaz and your immediate thought is that you are about to get a promotion at your job, there is a high chance that you'll be right.

Chapter 8: More Ways to Work with Runes

While most of the time, Norse runes are used for divinatory practices, they can also be a powerful addition to your meditation and magic rituals. You can select one or more runes associated with your intention for the rite and incorporate them into your practice. Not only that, but you can also wear them every day as a talisman to remind you of the intention you've set when charging the rune. This chapter covers several uses for runes - from meditation to making love talismans to Runic Reiki. Most of these options require you to use runic magic alongside other tools, which you are free to choose depending on what you feel you need to manifest your intention.

Using Runes in Rituals

Using runes in rituals requires regular practice because it increases focus and improves intuitive skills. The more you practice, the more vividly you can visualize runes, which, in turn, will significantly expand your ability to manifest your intent. The number of ways you can use runes in rituals is virtually limitless, as they can be incorporated into every type of ceremony. Here are a few simple ones to help you get started.

Rune Connection Empowering Exercise

Even if you've found the rune you feel drawn to and charged it with your energy, you may still want to strengthen your bond with it. Beginners can especially take advantage of this simple exercise. Here is how to perform this ritual:

- Cut out a 3x5 inch piece of paper and draw the rune you've chosen on it with a red marker.
- Sit in a comfortable position in front of your altar or table and place the paper in front of you.
- Take a couple of deep breaths while you focus on forming the rune in your mind.
- Repeat the name of the rune three times in your mind, or if you feel that it improves your concentration, you can also chant it out loud.
- Pause after the third time to see what the rune is telling you, then repeat its name three more times.
- Continue this for several minutes until you form a solid mental image of the shape of the rune - and its connection to the sensations running through your body and mind.
- The overall exercise should last no more than 10 minutes, but if you feel that you need more time to perfect your posture, breathing and focus, feel free to do it for as long as you want.

Ritual for Improving Your Focus

If you still have trouble maintaining your concentration, this exercise can help you improve this skill so you can manifest your intention. It's very similar to the previous one, except it focuses more on regulating breath patterns. Here is how to do it:

- Repeat the first step from the previous exercise up until you are getting ready to recite the name of the symbol.
- Here, you want to do this out loud while maintaining a specific breathing pattern. This involves inhaling for 10 seconds, holding your breath for 2 seconds, and releasing it along with the name of the symbol. Hold your breath once again for 2 seconds.
- Now, try shifting your position to see if it improves your concentration. For example, try standing up or laying down if you are sitting. If you were standing, sit down with your shoulders relaxed.

- Once you've found the position that works best for you, focus on the paper in front of you for a couple of minutes.
- Close your eyes and visualize the symbol in front of you. Try creating as vivid an image of it as possible.
- Once you can maintain the image in front of you for 10 minutes, you've successfully mastered this exercise.

Protection Ritual

Runic protection rituals were also popular among the ancient Norse. Apart from deterring negative influences from one's life, a protection ritual can also be performed to banish forces that may interfere with the work of the practitioner. Here is a protection rite you can practice every day and use in conjunction with any other ritual:

- Stand in a comfortable position and set a relaxing breathing rhythm. You can either follow the pattern described in the previous exercise or create your own.
- With your eyes closed or open, visualize either the Hagalaz or Eihwaz runes in red while chanting the sound out loud three times.
- Slowly turn in a circle while maintaining the image of the rune and repeating its name, and take on a steady and deep breathing rhythm.
- Once you can perform this exercise without breaks in your concentration, you will be able to undertake any other rune work with confidence.

Opening Ritual

In ancient times, powerful work with runic magic often required the practitioner to perform an invocatory ritual before the actual act. This helped prepare the practitioner's mind, body, and space for the process so they could manifest their intention more effectively. It typically also addresses a Norse deity who will be asked for assistance during the main ritual. If you wish to incorporate this ritual into your practice, you can do it by following this guide:

- Stand in the middle of a room or sacred space you've chosen to perform your ritual in, facing east or north.

- Holding the runes you'll be working with through the main ritual, recite the following:

  "Fare now mighty (the name of the Norse deity whom you are working with) from your heavenly home.

  Swiftly ride with all your might to help us give and gain.

  Holy runes we now use to draw the powers,

  the steady stream they flow with is now ours."

- Now walk to the most eastern or northern part of your space and, with your hand, trace a circle following the sun, left to right, while chanting:

  "These mighty runes are now drawn around us,

  unwanted forces; now stay away!"

- When you've completed the circle, return to the center of the space, facing the same direction as you did before. After that chant:

  "The worrisome forces are now on their way towards the east,

  hallowed be your name, oh mighty (name of Norse deity)."

- Once this invocatory ritual is completed, you can perform the primary rite.

Closing Ritual

When a magical act began with an opening ritual, the ancient Norse were also compelled to use a closing rite. This is used for the assimilation of messages received during the ritual and as an expression of gratitude for the help of the deities. This further fortifies the intent of the ritual. Here is how you can perform a successful closing ritual:

- Stand facing east or north while intoning:

  "Now the holy work is done with the help of (Norse deity).

  We hail to them because we know they granted us their help."

- Now, it's time for you to extinguish any candles or fire that's traditionally used during rituals.

- Hold or trace the Kenaz symbol and say the following:

- *"With the help of fire that's now ceased to glow, may forever be kindled with the mighty (Norse deity)."*

- If you've performed an empowering magic act, this may require you to internalize your newfound energy. So, the next step is to draw it in with the help of the Fehu rune.
- You can either hold this in your hand or draw its likeness in the air with your hand and take deep breaths.
- Draw your arms in, touching your solar plexus with your fingertips.
- Repeat this in all four cardinal directions, each time visualizing the energy being drawn into your center.
- With a last exhale of the exercise, let go of any images you've focused on during the rite and step away from the sacred space.

Runic Meditation

While a form of runic meditation has been covered in a previous chapter, this one brings a general type of meditation you can tailor to your preferences and magical needs.

Runic meditation can help you align your energy.
https://unsplash.com/photos/FjYwhowyp6k

Whichever magic act you decide to perform, this mediation can help you prepare for it by ensuring your energy is aligned with your needs. Here is how to do a runic meditation exercise:

- Find a quiet place where you won't be disturbed and are able to feel comfortable enough, and make this your dedicated meditation area.
- Using the symbols you feel drawn to at present, create a ring rune on a larger sheet of paper and place it in front of you so it'll be at eye level when meditating.
- Assume a comfortable position and take a few deep breaths.
- When you are relaxed enough, look at a rune ring in front of you.
- Now, you can step onto a secondary level of consciousness by placing the runes in the center of your focus.
- Concentrate on what the rune ring represents for you and how you plan to use it.
- Now, slowly close your eyes and continue visualizing the form of each rune as they appear on the paper.
- Contemplate their likeness in your mind's eye and listen to your intuition.
- If you are a beginner, you may have trouble focusing on the images with your eyes closed. If so, feel free to open your eyes and look at the symbols before closing them again.
- Having mastered the focus, you move on to a more complex analysis of the runes.
- In the beginning, you can maintain your focus on each rune for 10-15 seconds in an attempt to decipher them. After some practice, you'll be able to do this within 5 seconds per rune.
- After this, you should take a deep, cleansing breath and lapse into inner silence.
- During this, the runes you've visualized are being paired up with a resounding intent and purpose.
- You may continue the meditation as long as you feel a link with the runic force. In this meditative state, you may be led along numerous paths. Some will be associated with the rune itself, while others will reveal relationships between the runes. Either way, the possibilities for using runes meditation are infinite.

- Once you feel the link to the rune dissipating, you can end the meditation by taking a deep breath. If you wish, you can also repeat a closing statement similar to the following:

  "Now my work is done, and I am ready to go on."
- Open your eyes and break the ritual by stepping away from the meditation area.

Runic Talismans

Runes don't have to be limited to meditative or ritual uses. You can also benefit from their energy by wearing them as a talisman. With the symbol associated with what you want to achieve close to you, focusing on manifesting your intention in real life will be much easier.

Choose a rune that you really feel a connection with, as these will be in alignment with your intuition. Runic talismans are generally made from stone, wood, bone, or metal, although parchment paper was also used occasionally. Any one of these will work if you keep it on your desk or carry it around as a pendant.

The objects on which the runes are carved may also serve some utilitarian functions, such as pens, buckles, automobiles, and more. The following simple runic talismans and inscription formulas can be of help.

Encouraging or Binding Love

One of the most popular ways to use runes as talismans is to encourage love and affection to develop a relationship or strengthen the bond within an existing one. Remember that you can't create affection where there isn't any, and the runes should be used for good intentions. Apart from the ethical implications, love magic seems to work more effectively when it's used to enhance existing feelings. Here is how to create a talisman for love rituals:

- Create the runes by carving the following symbols into a piece of wood or stone:
- ᚷᚨᚾᛗᛞ
- Carve the name of the two people between whom you want to enhance the affection on the other side of the talisman.
- Whether you are making the talisman to enhance your love life or someone else's, make two sets so the spell can work on both

sides.
- After etching the names and symbols into the runes, you should charge the runes with your intention. Do this by focusing on the two people you want to bring together - as well as on the runic forces that'll bind the love.
- The two people the rune is meant for should wear the talisman close to their bodies to encourage affection from the other person. An alternate form of this ritual is etching the symbols into a pre-made piece of wooden or stone jewelry, which makes it easier to wear.
- The two parties can also place the talisman under each other's bed or over a threshold the other person regularly crosses.

Following a centuries-old tradition, practitioners of Norse magic often gift love charms to each other as part of their wedding ceremony. A modern take on this is for couples to express the strength of their bond by making elaborate invitations for wedding ceremonies, handfasting rituals, and any celebration they hold together.

Talisman for Wisdom

Talismans can also be used to gather wisdom. You will need a talisman, tools for making it, and a cup of wine or grape juice.

- If you are making the talisman by painting a rune onto it, make sure you use natural products instead of artificial coloring.
- If you are carving the runes, don't etch them too deeply into the surface either.
- While you can use several types of runes for a wisdom talisman, Mannaz works best to unlock new information for the conscious mind.
- Collect the shavings into a container and mix them with honey or mead. Repeat the following:

    "As I mix these runes, the sweet source of wisdom,

    They will blend together in a powerful bond."

    Take the cup into your hands and drink its content.
- Your energy is now absorbing inspiration and wisdom.

- You can wear the talisman or give it to someone who can benefit from the additional knowledge. The person wearing it will attract a wealth of information they can use to improve their lives.

Runic Healing and Reiki

Norse runes can also be used for healing, whether in Pagan-based or any other type of healing practice. An interesting use of runes for healing is combining them with the traditional Reiki symbols. This method is based on the Runic Reiki system, where both Norse and Reiki symbols are activated similarly, and the practitioner applies visualization to put them to use. What makes Runic Reiki so valuable is that it makes it easier to practice healing as it requires no hand placement as the traditional techniques do. This also makes Runic Reiki perfect for distance healing. Here is how to use this method:

- Start by visualizing the healing symbol to help diminish the effect of the distance between you and the recipient.
- Hold the Shai Nal Reiki symbol in your hands, as this will help you increase your power.
- Visualize tracing a line around the recipient's body with the Shai Nal symbol. It should start above their head and finish at their second chakra.
- Active Shail Nal by reciting its name three times in a row in your head.
- Within the lines of this symbol, you'll visualize a Norse rune associated with the body part you are trying to heal.
- For example, if you want to alleviate an emotional trauma, you will use Laguz. Whereas if you want to heal a physical injury or ailment, you will need to use Ehwaz. You can also use Mannaz to clear your mind and Uruz and Fehu to improve someone's health.
- Now, you should change your focus with the help of the Han-so symbol.
- Recite some position affirmations, such as:
  "You feel healthy and radiant."
  "You are not in pain."

- Statements that convey positive messages are easier for your subconscious to process, as it finds it harder to negative statements.
- Maintain the image of Shai Nal over the recipient and try to see them being surrounded by pink or red light.
- Use the Reloxone Reiki symbols to form a connection with a specific power source, like a Norse deity or any other guide you may use.
- When you have finished, seal your healing by visually combining the distance healing symbol with Algiz (for another layer of protection) or Sowilo (to thank your guide for allowing you to heal).

Chapter 9: Norse Magic in the Modern World

In modern times, Norse traditions are not directly related to the Vikings' beliefs. Due to the limited number of written sources on the subject, we have more of an interpretation of this old religion. Therefore, modern-day practitioners do what they feel is right for them.

Unlike most other religions, the Norse faith doesn't have one book with all the answers. Most followers will have a unique and individual way of doing things. The Poetic Edda, of course, is a wonderful resource that shows the original tales of the gods and their practices with runes and divination. But it's not going to give you everything you need to familiarize yourself with this religion.

For you to be able to develop your own method of practicing Norse magic, it is necessary to examine how modern-day practitioners use Norse magic and its traditions. The first thing you need to do is understand how Norse magic made its way into modern-day faith and how it has influenced the way we live. After that, you can decide if you want to practice individually or within a community, as there are just as many methods of community practice as there are independent ones. Following that, we will discuss a few ways in which you can incorporate Norse magic into your daily life and make it part of your everyday routine.

Ásatrú (Ásatrúarfélagið)

The Old Norse paganism Ásatrú, the religion of the original Viking settlers, is going through a renaissance of sorts. Spiritual paths rooted in the Norse ancestors' practices and beliefs are common in modern society. Some Norse Pagans refer to themselves as Heathens, but many refer to themselves as Asatru.

Asatru was the name created by Nordic Neo-pagans during the Middle Ages. This term was coined in the 19th century to describe the reconstruction of the religious traditions of Scandinavia from before Christianity was introduced. In this time period, the 19th century, Asatru roughly translated as "to be true to the Aesir," one of the Norse God tribes (Odin, Höðr, Baldr, Frigg, Thor, Freyr, and Freyja). Aesir, the main group of the Norse Gods, became the focus of the Asatru religion. The term refers to a set of religions and spiritualities that originates from Northern European spiritual beliefs.

Asatru concept then refers to being faithful to the Norse gods while also recognizing pagan traditions from the pre-Christian Scandinavian era, leading to the creation of new branches of this faith.

Modern-Day Ásatrú

Sveinbjorn Beinteinsson played an essential role in establishing Asatru's recognition by the Icelandic government in 1972 during the late 1960s and early 1970s. At this point, several Asatru organizations began to appear throughout Europe and America. Many people worldwide follow Asatru, primarily in organizations in the United States and Europe, and it is even recognized as an official religion in certain European countries.

There is a great emphasis on Norse myths in Asatru, even though they are not considered historical facts. Instead, they are seen as a guide to achieving greatness, enjoying the world, and utilizing everything around us to our advantage. We humans have an intimate relationship with the gods since they are often seen as part of nature. However, we only turn to the gods for help when all human efforts, resources, and every single other option have been exhausted. Worshiping the Norse gods calls for a gift. As a result, sacrifices are often made in the form of ceremonies in which food, drink, and personal items are shared. This is done to maintain a strong bond between the gods and us.

According to the adherents of the Asatru tradition, objects are considered to be an important part of the connection between human beings and the gods. There is a possibility that objects can be infused with power by the gods. It is believed that all things within the universe are connected to each other by a flow of energy. As an example, we may create a rune charm or divination set. In a sense, we are binding our essence to it. By giving it shape, we give it a part of ourselves and, as an offering, we can give this to the gods. In exchange, the gods provide us with power and enthusiasm that will help us live our lives on our own. The gods are manifestations of spiritual reality, which, in turn, affects us.

Followers of Asatru do not pray to the Gods. Instead of relying on formal rites, they meditate and seek their blessings through informal rituals. This aspect of honor is in itself a form of prayer to live a good and moral life and expresses the love of freedom because it is non-authoritarian and decentralized. Asatru has no all-powerful spiritual leader dictating truth to the world. There is no direct connection between a guru or priest and the Gods; instead, it is believed that the gods are a part of you.

Ásatrú as an Organization

The religion does, however, have some hierarchies based on specific organizations. An Asatru organization is known as a Kindred. A Kindred's priests are known as Gothar, which is a plural form of Gothi or Gythia. A Gothar is the Asatru community's collective priesthood, and Folk is its congregation. Like many pagan religions, this one emphasizes community as an essential aspect of its practice. Each member of the community has an important role to play in forming a unified force that benefits the whole. This way, the community is protected, fertile, prosperous, and well-off.

The Gothar are the collective priesthood of the Asatru Community. It translates to those who speak the godly tongue. A member of the Gothar is a highly visible member of the greater Asatru Community. People who wish to become Gothar must possess three things: Odin's wisdom, Thor's strength, and Freyja's love. Asatru worships these three primary deities. The three aspects are often expressed through sacred texts, belonging to a kindred and caring for the folk. In addition to guiding the folk with wisdom, being strong for the community and working for the benefit of the community requires a certain amount of love, friendship, and compassion. They are generally expected to conduct themselves in a way that sets an excellent example for others to follow. They play an essential role in the legacy and history of those who practice Asatru. The Althing, a high council of Asatru, sets the bylaws that the Folk must adhere to. Speakers of the Althing, the prominent voice of the council, are chosen by their kindred.

Asatru is a religion that shapes itself to modern needs and, as such, many Asatru organizations may do things differently, but the canons of this religion are the aforementioned basics.

Different Ásatrú Organizations

There is a wondrous variety of modern-day Asatru spiritualities based on pagan traditions. Asatru is the most famous neo-pagan branch, and there are differences from organization to organization. For example, one will focus solely on the Aesir, that is, Odin, Höðr, Baldr, Frigg, Thor, Freyr, and Freyja; sky gods, war gods, law, justice, poetry, and wisdom. Others are more focused on social realities and the need to maintain order with emphasis on fertility, prosperity, plenty, and magic.

In other words, Asatru is a neo-pagan polytheistic reconstruction based on certain religious and historical aspects of pre-Christian Scandinavia, a revival of the pre-Christian indigenous religion of the Norse people.

The followers of this faith, however, acknowledge that other people have their own gods as well as interacting with the Norse gods. It is important to note that Asatru followers do not believe that their gods represent the only true gods. No hierarchical structures, dogmas, or sacred books are at the center of the religion, which is a reconstruction of a religious tradition. Due to this, religious practices may differ in interpretation based on their environment.

Odinism

Odinism is another form of Norse theology organization. It's named after the god Odin. Reconstructed in modern times as a religion concerned with Germanic paganism, runes, mythology, and folklore. The first mention of Odinism dates back to the 1820s. In 1840, the term was used by Thomas Carlyle, a Scottish essayist, historian, and philosopher. Those who practice Odinism are associated with pagans and even white supremacists. Those who practice under Odin are often seen wearing a pendant with Thor's hammer around their necks.

Across Europe and parts of America, Odinism would continue to be practiced and altered ever since its inception. Today, there is very little research about Odinism because it has been erased and changed throughout history. Especially as Christianity made its way through the world. When Christianity came through, they heavily shunned paganism of any kind, including Odinism.

In the mid-1970s, the Committee for the Restoration of the Odinic Rite or Odinist Committee was founded in Britain. It represents a modern-day revival of Norse magical practices under the term Odinism. In 1980, the organization changed its name to The Odinic Rite following the increased interest in restoring the Odinic faith.

Modern Odinism beliefs are polytheistic, meaning they believe in more than one deity. The Viking era represents just a tiny portion of the evolution and history of the Odinic Rite. They disdain terms like Viking religion or Asatru.

According to the Odinic Rite, members should live according to the Nine Noble Virtues, based on writing found in the Poetic Edda like The Sigrdrífomál and The Hávamál:

- Self-reliance
- Perseverance
- Discipline
- Honor
- Courage
- Industriousness
- Hospitality
- Fidelity
- Truth

Modern Day Practice of Norse Magic

There is a general consensus that magic can be divided into good magic and evil magic. As common as this is among general populations, it is also prevalent in theories. The pre-Christian Germanic peoples, however, had fundamentally different ideas about magic and used it in various ways. As a result, modern magic involves tuning oneself in to nature and discerning fate to accomplish one's goals.

Going It Alone

The fact that there is no one way to practice is compelling to many followers. You have to discover everything for yourself. But it is through this self-discovery and research that you're going to learn and become a better version of yourself. As you go along this path, you may discover that there is a lot of alone time involved. Unlike other organizations, there is a lack of community-based learning and practice involved. Solitary worship of the gods and divination practice take place alone because it's a nature-based religion, one that involves personal growth and self-exploration. It is also an exploration of a relationship with the gods, so you will spend a lot of time with candles, fires, books, and runes. Learning more about the gods and the faith ties heavily into practice and research.

Community

Despite this solitary aspect of Modern day Norse practice, a knowledgeable community exists. Once you know how to find your fellow practitioners, you can start learning more and more. Meeting others that have had unique experiences and talking and learning from them is possible. Social media is a great way to connect with others who share your beliefs and interests. Other practitioners meet up to attend gatherings, and the community aspect of their respective religions can inspire you to continue on your path of divination, magic, and faith.

Gatherings

The old Nordic religion is still practiced openly - just like it was during the Viking age. Some practitioners praise and make offerings, toasts are drunk, and feasts are eaten to honor them. While some individuals will wish for prosperity and health by toasting the fertility gods Frej and Njörd, others can invoke Odin for wisdom or praise Thor for strength when facing a challenge. Some Nordic believers will gather in groups and go to specific sites to worship the gods and their magic. They will make offerings at pre-Christian cult sites to feel the power of their ancestors. Among the possible locations are Bronze Age burial mounds or Viking Age ship settings. There is usually a ceremonial circle formed between the participants. Within the circle, this creates a "holy space" that connects to the gods' world. The circle is then ceremonially closed again after the participants have paid their respects to their gods. A total of four offerings are brought to the altar each year during the summer, solstice, winter solstice, autumn solstice, and spring equinox.

These group meetings are usually made up of individual practitioners. But there are organizations like Odinism and Asatru that hold weekly services.

Daily Practices to Incorporate into Your Life

In Norse-related activities, each individual worships the gods and nature in their own way. Whichever method works best for them is correct.

Amulets and Charms

Amulets have been used for thousands of years.
https://unsplash.com/photos/rsjwsaTLGgE

For thousands of years, people have worn specific Norse-related jewelry as a way to signify their faith. And to this day, there are thousands of people around the world who do the same thing. Whether in the form of Mjölnir (Thor's hammer) or rune charms, it's a powerful method to help reflect on what these things symbolize; Thor's guidance for strength but also the protection of the gods and your honor to them.

Nature

Take 10 or 15 minutes to sit outside every day. No matter what the weather, observe the world around you and really think about your faith. Because nature is such an essential aspect of this faith, finding a place you can escape to for just a few minutes every day will make a massive difference in how you connect with it. You need nature to separate you from the outside world. Whether it's a single tree, a bush, a patch of grass, or even a potted plant in your home, find somewhere that you can just disappear and reconnect to nature, even for a few minutes.

Don't Expect Results Straight Away

By adhering to the Norse traditions' beliefs, you will have these big moments of realization and awareness. They may not happen every day or every week. They may not even happen every month. For the most part, we live our lives as we normally do, but it is still possible to bring a little bit more faith and rhythm into them with each little step we make toward understanding these complex traditions. So, it's important not to expect too much too soon. The big moments will come when they're meant to. The gods will show you the signs when you're meant to see them. And in the meantime, there is nothing wrong with enjoying a little bit of peace to sit back and enjoy nature and take note of the small signs in everyday life.

Indoor Altar

Another great way to incorporate the Norse traditions into your life is by creating an indoor altar. It can be in any style or size you want. Some people will have a Thor figure, along with some herbs, candles, and incense. While others will fill their table with their runes, charms, and crystals. This allows practitioners to feel connected to the gods while away from home. It can create tremendous strength and determination throughout the day to know they are there when you get home. You could also build an outdoor altar to represent your attachment to the natural world. Maintaining your altar and keeping it clean and organized while decorating it in any way you like is a great way to connect with your faith and the magical possibilities it can provide.

A shrine can just as easily be included in an offering to the gods. Spending time in front of your shrine or altar for the gods, ancestors, or spirits and meditating can help you feel connected to it.

Our previous discussion has emphasized the importance of the small details in your Norse venture. It is not possible for us to hunt a wild boar for sacrifice to Odin like the Vikings or our pagan ancestors. So, making these small offerings is an honorable way to pay homage to the history of Norse tradition, even if we cannot do it on a large scale.

There are various ways you can stay connected and get an extra moment to reflect on your journey. If you have anything you do that you believe might be helpful to others, or if you just want to share your story or share your daily rituals as a Norse Pagan, you can share them with the world. Creating a platform to tell your tale, whether it is on social media, a website, or in a book, can be great ways to learn from your experiences and inspire others along the way. Being able to stay connected outside of those important moments of life is one of the most challenging disciplines of this faith.

Having read this chapter on the traditions of Norse magic and its uses in modern society, you have taken one of the most important steps along your magical journey. There is no doubt that this will help you expand your spiritual horizons, and you will have a better understanding of other spiritual realities, which, in turn, will help you to take that step forward, go over the fence, and gradually leap into the possibilities of Norse magic.

Bonus: List of Runes and Their Symbolism

In this section, you will find a quick reference guide to all of the Elder Futhark runes. Listed are the names of the runes, the Aetts they belong to, and their corresponding places within each Aett. You can refer back to this page whenever you need a refresher on the pronunciation of rune names or the meaning of their magical symbolism.

Aettir (plural form of aett) is the term used to divide the Elder Futhark runes into three equal parts. The division enables students to study in a structured manner. Before moving on to the next aett, many people like to understand the previous one better. The themes of each Aett are different, but there are also some commonalities. While each aett is singularly unique on its own, they each also represent luminosity in one way or another. All three Aett have a rune that represents wealth in some way and at least one that represents danger.

The First Aett: Freya's Aett

The first Aett belongs to Freya, the Norse goddess of beauty, fertility, and love. This collection of runes is about enjoyment, love, emotions, happiness, and physical presence. It also refers to creation, growth, and beginnings.

Freya's Aett represents the nurturer, the mother, the farmer, and the merchant. It is also the Aettir of the first degree as it represents the cycle of life.

In Freyr's Aett, the runes represent what it takes to live a fulfilling life, to experience and interact with other humans, and to experience the divine.

FEHU

Letter Value: F

English Pronunciation: "FAY-hoo"

Translation: Cattle, prosperity, property, hope, happiness, abundance, wealth, and financial gain.

Magical Symbolism: Achieve goals, luck, new beginnings, abundance, success, luck.

In Practice: Focus its energies where you wish to experience the most success in your life, as it represents abundance, achievement, and prosperity.

URUZ

Letter Value: U

English Pronunciation: "OO-rooz"

Translation: Wild ox, unexpected change, life force, indomitability, strength, power, and good mental and physical health.

Magical Symbolism: Understanding, strength, speed, energy, courage, dedication, vitality.

In Practice: Uruz helps to shape the world around you. It can guide you both physically and mentally and can refer to many aspects of change – it could mean that you will have more strength or that you are going to be challenged in your strength. Uruz also deals with your past strength – your health and actions coming back to haunt you.

THURISAZ

Letter Value: TH

English Pronunciation: "THUR-ee-sazh"

Translation: Giant, god of Thunder, lightning, thorn, caution, defensive force, and disruption.

Magical Symbolism: Focus on getting rid of the negative, regeneration, concentration, and self-discipline.

In Practice: Thurisaz is both sides of the same coin - it can be about protection, but the same force that protects can also destroy. The name comes from "Thor," the god of lightning, and we know from legend that he can destroy as much as he can create.

ANSUZ

Letter Value: A

English Pronunciation: "AHN-sooz"

Translation: The All Father, Odin, and the other gods are represented by "A." It means wisdom, life, communing, mouth, listening, and prophecy.

Magical Symbolism: Leadership, communication, wisdom, signals, health.

In Practice: Ansuz is linked to Odin and the ancestral gods. It represents wise communication and well-intended listening- to yourself and others.

RAIDHO

Letter Value: R

English Pronunciation: "Rah-EED-ho"

Translation: Travel & change, rest & rhythm, journeying, wagon, momentum, the big picture.

Magical Symbolism: Bring about change, protection for travelers, rhythm, facilitate change, and reconnect.

In Practice: Raidho is the contemplation of achieving something and the discipline to follow through with it. This rune is the power to move forward toward our desired destinations.

KENAZ

Letter Value: K/C

English Pronunciation: "KEN-nahz"

Translation: Fire, energy, torch or beacon, light, passion, transform, and creation.

Magical Symbolism: Light, motivation, regeneration, inspiration, regeneration.

In Practice: As a torch, Kenaz illuminates the way through the darkness. Kenaz is the controlled energy or burning flame that can create and transform. When you look inside, you can find Kenaz – your burning passion. When you focus on your burning passion, you can keep out negative influences.

GEBO

Letter Value: G

English Pronunciation: "GHEH-boh"

Translation: Togetherness, gifting, generous, exchange, gratitude, giving & receiving, sacrifice (self), forgiving, and offering.

Magical Symbolism: Balance, luck, fertility, successful partnering, giving.

In Practice: The giving or receiving of a gift is represented by Gebo. We should receive a gift as well as we give one, and there should be no expectations about what we are about to receive or the other person's role in the process.

WUNJO

Letter Value: W

English Pronunciation: "WOON-yo"

Translation: Harmony, Fullness, joy, wellbeing, alignment, contentment, ecstasy, and balance.

Magical Symbolism: Happiness, harmony, joy, prosperity, success, motivation.

In Practice: Wunjo represents fulfilling goals. Whenever we are in harmony with our goals and working together, we will prosper and grow.

The Second Aett: Hagal's Aett

The Second Aett, Hagal, represents the forces that surround us. In most cases, these are not governed by intelligence – but by the forces of nature.

Hagal is a warrior. He shows unending courage and tenacity despite overwhelming odds. The key components of this Aett are money, accomplishments, power, victories, and success. A force outside our control is present in Hagal.

Neutrality is its defining characteristic. It is the runes of Hagal's Aett which speak to the unexpected occurrences in life, such as disruptions, changes, stalled progress, and unforeseen good fortune. Nothing lasts forever, so they help us get through the more challenging parts of our lives.

HAGALAZ

Letter Value: H

English Pronunciation: "HA-ga-lahz"

Translation: Hail, destruction, sudden difficulties, violent change of nature, and delay.

Magical Symbolism: Destructive, dangerous weather, breaking destructive patterns, the wrath of nature, uncontrolled forces.

In Practice: Hagalaz is about being patient and witting for what is coming your way. There might be obstacles, challenges, and delays, and you must accept this delay and disruption, content that it is part of your change and journey.

NAUTHIZ

Letter Value: N

English Pronunciation: "NOWD-heez"

Translation: Need, distress, desire for triumph, stagnation, and change manifestation.

Magical Symbolism: Survival, frustration, endurance, obstacles, determination.

In Practice: Naudhiz is a manifestation of distress, struggle, and need, but it is also a manifestation of overcoming those challenges.

ISA

Letter Value: I

English Pronunciation: "EEH-sah"

Translation: Cold, winter, ice, change, momentum, still, delay, waiting, new beginnings, and pauses.

Magical Symbolism: Reinforcement of other kinds of magic, ice, obstacles, blockages, freezing, reflection.

In Practice: Isa is the calm before the storm, the stillness that comes from the change in your life. When we feel we are stagnating, we are often not, and Isa is our old ways and habits that are ingrained into our minds. We need the stagnation to bring about the change.

JERA

Letter Value: J / Y

English Pronunciation: "YAR-ah"

Translation: Cycles, circles, time, movement, rewards, value, harvesting what has been sown, and the prize of our efforts.

Magical Symbolism: Fruition, eliminate stagnation, growth, harvest, create change.

In Practice: Night gives way to day. There are new cycles all around us, like dawn after the dark. A new cycle has begun, and with Jera, you are rewarded for your hard work put in.

EIHWAZ

Letter Value: E / I

English Pronunciation: "EYE-wahz"

Translation: The great yew tree, long life, wisdom, life & death, sacrifice, new beginnings, and moving on to the next stage.

Magical Symbolism: To ease a life transition, defense, transformation, protection, cause change.

In Practice: Eihwaz symbolizes the yew tree, which represents life and death. This death, however, is not always literal. Transitions can be signified by it. Closing the door to allow another to open. To move forward, you have to leave the past in the past.

PERTHRO

Letter Value: P

English Pronunciation: "PEHR-throw"

Translation: What is to come, mysteries, the hidden, secrets, the self, what is inside, fate, and casting.

Magical Symbolism: Knowledge of secrets, fertility, enhancing self and powers, control of uncertainty.

In Practice: Perthro represents Karma. Our current situation is a result of the actions we or someone else have taken in the past. It aids with contemplation.

ALGIZ

Letter Value: Z

English Pronunciation: "AHL-geez"

Translation: Luck, defense, good omens, elks, instinct & self-protection, safe haven, and the connection to what is more than you.

Magical Symbolism: Channeling energy, a shield, protection, ward against evil, guardian.

In Practice: Algiz is a force of protection. It can be a sign that one needs to seek refuge. Algiz is also an omen of luck, strengthening awareness and bringing guidance to those who need it.

SOWILO

Letter Value: S

English Pronunciation: "Soh-WEE-low"

Translation: Power, spirit, strength, health & vitality, enlightenment, energy, goodness, success, and your growth.

Magical Symbolism: Cosmic force, energy, healing, strength, cleansing, success.

In Practice: Sowilo cuts through the darkness and your own self-doubts – giving you the chance to grow and change, to expand to be the person you know you can be. You can find your purpose and look toward your ultimate goal.

The Third Aett: Tyr's Aett

This third set of runes addresses the internal forces we encounter as we travel the path outlined in the First Aett and deal with the external forces of the Second Aett.

As a symbol of victory and protection, Tyr symbolizes moral values, justice, spiritual attainment, understanding, atonement, establishing order, and all matters involving authority and politics. It focuses on intellectual development, understanding, and spiritual growth.

There are direct connections between the runes of Tyr's Aett and ancient deities, natural forces, and humanity itself, illustrating aspects of the dance between visible and invisible realms.

TIWAZ

Letter Value: T

English Pronunciation: "TEE-wahz"

Translation: The God Tyr, victory, bravery, courage, need for justice, honor, and sacrifice for the greater good.

Magical Symbolism: Victory, protection, reinforced will, strength, healing a wound, analysis.

In Practice: Tiwaz is a symbol of facing opposition with courage and is a direct influence from the Norse god of war and bloodshed, Tyr. Tiwaz means strength and fearlessness.

BERKANA

Letter Value: B

English Pronunciation: "BEHR-kah-nah"

Translation: New beginnings & rebirth, a change, new phases in life, relationships, projects, the birch tree, and the cycles of life.

Magical Symbolism: Starting again, encouragement, desire, healing, regeneration, liberation.

In Practice: Symbolizing life's transitions, Berkano represents growth and a new beginning. Berkano reminds us that every ending brings a fresh beginning, and every phase brings its own challenges and celebrations.

EHWAZ

Letter Value: E

English Pronunciation: "EH-wahz"

Translation: Partnership & cooperation, horses, loyalty, moving forward, progress, and workmen together.

Magical Symbolism: Energy, power, trust, progress, communication, progress, change, transportation.

In Practice: Ehwaz represents a collaborative effort to incite change and progress. Trust and loyalty are essential for successful relationships between partners or between the conflicting parts of ourselves.

MANNAZ

Letter Value: M
English Pronunciation: "MAN-az"

Translation: Divine & human potential, wisdom, intelligence, reasoning, traditions & habits, self-development, balance, and reason.

Magical Symbolism: Order in life, intelligence, thought, ability, skill, create.

In Practice: Mannaz symbolizes intelligence, rationality, and tradition. The pursuit of a perfect balance in life is self-development. The Mannaz rune can help you increase rational thought and gain control over your emotions.

LAGUZ

Letter Value: L
English Pronunciation: "LAH-good"

Translation: Water, intuition, flow, cleansing, inward journey, personality depth.

Magical Symbolism: Stabilize emotions and turmoil, enhance psychic abilities, uncover the truth, and confront fears.

In Practice: All life comes from water, which is represented by Laguz. In the same way, water symbolizes our emotional journey and the flow of our lives. Through it, we can deal with difficult growth and transition through life's transitions.

INGWAZ

Letter Value: NG
English Pronunciation: "ING-wahz"

Translation: Sexuality, fertility, self-development, energy, potential, family, ancestors, and doing things at the right time.

Magical Symbolism: Strength, growth, health, balance, grounded, connect.

In Practice: Potential energy is represented by Ingwaz. A reminder that things cannot be rushed. The rune helps you to prepare for what is to come, so you have the energy ready to be transformed – aiding your patience and building your strength.

DAGAZ

Letter Value: D

English Pronunciation: "DAH-gahz"

Translation: Immediate change, the coming light, the illumination of the gods, self-betterment, inspiration, wisdom, the day.

Magical Symbolism: Clarity, positivity, awakening, awareness, transformation.

In Practice: A new era begins with Dagaz, which represents divine inspiration and the end of an era. By going with the flow and enjoying the beauty of life, you will find your muse all around you.

OTHALA

Letter Value: O

English Pronunciation: "Oh-THA-la"

Translation: Spirit, wisdom, intelligence, talent, welcoming, community, people, ancestors, physical buildings, and finding your roots.

Magical Symbolism: Influence over possessions, inheritance, experience, ancestry, heritage, and value.

In Practice: We have a legacy with Othala. We all have both the material and spiritual around us. OTHALA represents the spiritual and material assets we have attained. We must use Othala to better build and grow our lives.

Part 2: Trolldom

Unlocking the Traditional Magic Practice of Sweden, Norway, Denmark, and Finland

Introduction

The frozen north doesn't sound like the most magical place on Earth, but this is where we need to go to discover the magic of trolldom and Norse mythology. It has always been an unforgiving place with a harsh climate and hardy people, but maybe these facts make the Nordic ways so compelling. They had to survive their environment and thrive, so the stories that accompanied their history became increasingly enchanting and filled with heroes, heroines, gods and goddesses, and a series of magical beings they needed to defeat to become victorious.

These stories are inspiring and exciting. Bloodthirsty and violent, they also contain all the emotional ups and downs to keep people interested and engaged. The practices of the Nordic folk are what we are going to concentrate on and find a way to connect to these ancient people. The rituals and potions they used have been developed to fit modern times and can be used to make your own form of magic. Why do you need trolldom or any type of magical influence in your life? Maybe you don't need them, but why wouldn't you want them? Broaden your mind and knowledge, and get ready to welcome Nordic ways into your life.

Chapter 1: Introducing Trolldom

Trolls are generally thought of as cute neon-haired dolls that sit on your desk and are fun to collect. They appear in modern culture, and thanks to the fantasy genre, they have played a part in many movies and books. From the dark, evil creatures featured in J.R.R. Tolkien's sagas to the cute Disney trolls with ribbons in their hair, we have all encountered trolls in one form or another, but what do we really know about them?

They are mythical creatures who have appeared in ancient texts as far back as Norse times, but they probably existed long before. The origin of the name troll has been a cause of disagreement for many experts, and some believe it is derived from the Norse word Jotunn who were giants who inhabited the world before the dawn of humankind. The trolldom we will be considering is a Germanic word that means witchcraft and the practices associated with this particular form of spell work.

We will concentrate on the Scandinavian and Germanic beliefs surrounding trolls and their importance for trolldom. One of the most recognizable tales from Scandinavia featuring the creatures is the story of Three Billy Goats Gruff, in which a fearsome troll guards the bridge the three goats need to cross. The goats are all assorted sizes, sending the smallest goat across the bridge first. The troll threatens to eat the small goat, but it tells the troll if he waits, a larger and more filling meal will come soon. The troll agrees and lets the small goat pass. The second goat then crosses and is stopped by the troll, threatening to eat him. The second goat tells him that a larger goat is coming, which will mean a bigger meal for the troll. The troll agrees and lets him pass. When the third goat attempts to cross the bridge, it calls the troll's bluff and dares him to eat him up. When the troll attacks, the goat knocks him off the bridge with his huge horns, and the troll is swept away by the river. The bridge is now safe for all to pass, and the three goats live happily ever after.

This cautionary tale about greed and being happy with what you have has been a popular children's story since Hans Christian Anderson was introduced to the UK in 1859. A series of Scandinavian and Danish tales have been the staple reading for children ever since.

Some experts believe the troll was part of Prehistoric culture because of cave drawings and other artwork from that age, and the memory of them from Cro-Magnon times has filtered down to Northern Europe as man began to migrate the world. This theory doesn't work for experts who believe trolls originated in Scandinavia because, during that era, a large glacier covered the area that is today known as Scandinavia.

These theories show trolls as part of the forefather cult belief prevalent in the tenth and eleventh centuries – when Scandinavians believed in the power of the dead and ancestors were encouraged to return to the living world and share their powers. The believers would sit on mounds to communicate with the deceased and make contact. When Christianity became popular in Europe, laws were passed to make the practices illegal, and those beliefs were considered evil and dangerous.

This theory also fits with the Norse culture in which trolls were classed as the spirits of the dead who would often visit the living and help them or return to wreak their revenge on those who had caused them harm during their time on Earth. The trolls of Scandinavia and Norway are scary creatures living in mountains and forests and are huge, even giant-sized, and they work with the natural elements surrounding them. Others are shorter and live in caves or underground lairs. They usually have scraggy and unkempt hair, large noses, and sharp teeth. Some even have multiple heads and tails to make their appearance more intimidating.

Trolldom

The magic associated with the Scandinavian and Norwegian areas still exists today, and some natives even claim to believe in the existence of real trolls. They tell their children stories of these legendary creatures who will escape their natural dwellings to seek out children who have been badly behaved and eat them! In Iceland, there are a series of thirteen troll sons of the famous Gryla who visit children for thirteen days before Christmas and leave a gift for good children and rotting vegetables for naughty children. They are known as the Yule Boys and have become part of the tourist attractions found in the Nordic area.

The magic of trolldom is based on nature and the power of sunlight especially. Because the area has short periods of sunlight, and the dark is a constant state for most people, the power of solar energy is more significant. It has been compared to Norse magic, the pagan spells and working of Wiccans, and the rituals and spells of Hoodoo. All these practices are based on helping people and improving circumstances, although there are some rituals and spells that can cause harm. Magic is a personal choice, and trolldom lets you take aspects from traditional Nordic practices and intersperse them with elements from African American, English, and Germanic folk magic to create a unique cultural practice.

Spells Included in Trolldom

Using the term "root work" to describe magic gives you a more detailed insight into what the results should be. Spells and potions, rituals, and conjuring should be used to get to the root of your problems and heal them. What is wrong with your love life, or why has your career ground to a halt? Are you unlucky, or could you use some help in legal matters? Some magic is more general and can be used to alter all-encompassing circumstances, while other magic is used to address more definitive problems.

When the people living in the Nordic regions needed help, there were very few options to consider. They lived in small communities and relied heavily upon the magic practices of their culture. When their crops failed, or their children were taken ill, or disappeared, it seemed logical to turn to mythological creatures to seek reasons why these awful things were happening. Today we know that circumstances happen because of forces we can't control mixed with influences that result from our actions. Or, as some people like to say, "sh#t happens", but imagine if your world was so restricted that you believed that trolls and other mythical creatures influenced what happened in your life. How frightening would that be? It is no wonder that magic and the effect it was perceived to have had such a significant effect on everyday life. Pagan heathenry today means that practitioners adapt to nature and its wonders with more modern practices to reconnect to the world and regain some of the power that seems to have been taken away from us by religion, government, and societal taboos.

Why Is Nordic Magic So Relevant Today?

Consider how traditional religions and society dictate how we should live. There are strict rules and ideals to live up to and harsh judgments for those who don't adhere. Should we be forced to live with such exacting rules and beliefs? More and more people are bucking the trend and embracing a belief that it's okay to be different. Nonconformity is becoming the norm (oh, the irony!), which includes embracing magic and mythology from the past. Nordic mythology is different; it is filled with flawed characters who had faults and were definitely imperfect. They made mistakes, and they were punished. They had unusual love lives and relationships, and they lived colorful lives filled with drama, romance, love, lust, and war.

The beliefs and practices of the Nordic people weren't just mythical, and we can look to the past for proof that this was how they lived their lives. Relics, artifacts, and physical proof of their civilization have been found and have been adopted by modern practitioners to show allegiance to the Nordic ways. Trolldom is a part of the overall belief system based on magic connected to trolls, elves, and dwarves. These mythical beings played an intrinsic role in the lives of the gods and goddesses of the time and influenced their lives hugely.

This book will show you how to cast spells and make potions that have transcended from history to become part of the magic workings performed today. The knowledge of trolldom gives you a deeper understanding of how ingredients and rituals work to influence the power you have over your and other people's lives. Medieval magic doesn't mean it is less effective than modern work. In fact, it is considered more potent because it has survived so long. Magic is often passed down through generations and is improved, adapted, and expanded.

The problems we face today may seem different from the past, but they aren't! We all want better lives, we all face negative forces, and we all have relationship issues. Use trolldom magic, elven and dwarf magic to use your powers to achieve positive outcomes. As you develop your skills, you'll be blessed with a greater understanding of the power of nature and how to harness it.

Imagine your life filled with quests and adventures. New horizons and destinations await you, and the Norse folk magic will keep you safe and ensure you are successful. Using candle magic, sun, moon magic, herbal, crystal, and magical tools, you'll become adept at Norse folk magic and its benefits. Bring the Nordic culture into your lives and celebrate the magic it holds. Holidays and celebrations will become even more special when you embrace trolldom and Norse ways.

Symbols and Rituals

The Valknut symbol.
https://commons.wikimedia.org/wiki/File:9crossings-knot-symmetric-triangles-quasi-valknut.svg

Norse magic uses the power of symbols to strengthen its potency. The easiest way to start your work with trolldom is to incorporate some powerful Norse symbols into your life. Use these examples to decorate your home or personal space and become familiar with Norse magic and its powers.

- **The Valknut** is a prominent and powerful representation of the god Odin. It comprises three triangles forming nine points, all surrounded by a circle. The nine points represent the nine worlds in Norse mythology, while the circle represents the perpetuity of humankind through motherhood and birth.
- **Yggdrasil** is the great tree of the world. It is a giant tree with deep roots representing the universe and how we are all connected. The branches connect the nine realms and deliver life-saving water through their boughs. At the end of the world, or Ragnarök, the gods and their enemies will battle it out until all existence is destroyed. There will be a single man and a woman

hiding in the trunk of Yggdrasil who will emerge and repopulate the world.

- **The Helm of Awe** is an eight-sided symbol surrounded by a circle of dragon-like creatures joined by their tails. It was drawn on the foreheads of warriors to protect them in battle. Today it is used in tattoo form to give protection or to signal that the wearer is a believer in Asatru, the Viking and Norse religion.

- **The Triple Horn of Odin** is a symbol formed by three horns interlocked to form a solid form surrounded by a circle of decorative runes or leaves, depending on the designer. The story behind the horns is based on the myth that tells the story of two dwarves named Fjalar and Galar, who were so knowledgeable they could answer any question in the universe. They killed the first being known as Kvasir and mixed his blood with honey – a mixture used to fill three horns, and he blessed one of them with the Mead of Poetry. Odin was desperate to drink the mead and made a pact with the mighty giant Gunnloo to take a sip from each for three days. He tricked her and drank the whole horn, which made him turn into an eagle and escape. The symbol represents wisdom and poetic inspiration.

- **The Mjolnir** is also known as the hammer of Thor and was forged by a dwarf. It wasn't just a tool or weapon. It was also used to consecrate marriages and provide the couple with fertility. It is a symbol of strength and protection and was used by other religions in conjunction with the more traditional cross symbol. It is represented by a decorative hammer-shaped symbol, often with the head facing downward.

- **The Swastika** was a Viking/Norse symbol that the Nazi Party seriously misused in the 1930s. Originally it was used to bring prosperity and order to a person who was experiencing chaos and distress. It is considered one of the most significant good luck charms of Norse beliefs but should only be displayed in places where this knowledge is freely available. Don't forget that the swastika can be considered offensive by some because of its history.

- **The Troll Cross** is a circle with two small horns underneath. It is designed to protect the wearer from the dark practices of elves, trolls, and dwarves.

- The three triangles of Odin are a recurring theme in Nordic symbolism. They have multiple meanings and can be used to represent the following:
- **The Three Roots of Yggdrasil** and the connection to the nine realms.
- **The Three Realms** existed before the earth's creation and man's time on the physical plane. There was a land of fire and land of mist and an indistinct space between the two.
- **The Three Grandchildren of Buri**, the first God of Norse mythology – who was licked out of a block of ice by a mythical cow named Audhumla. His son didn't have much effect on Norse tales, but he produced three sons named Odin, Vili, and Ve. They are attributed to bringing life and senses to humankind and improving their existence on Earth.
- **The Three Goddesses of Fate**. Each one represents the past, the future, and the present.
- Symbols surround us and affect our everyday life. Everybody recognizes the golden archway representing a certain burger joint and what the swish on the side of a good pair of trainers means. Advertisers and big companies are merely trading on ancient knowledge, which means one symbol or sign could be more significant than a hundred words. We gain comfort, strength, and protection from things that represent familiarity, and Norse signs work similarly.

Call it what you like, shamanism, heathenry, Asatru, Wiccan, or pagan; these types of magic and beliefs are experiencing a renaissance for a reason. More people are becoming disillusioned with modern life and are turning to the more traditional methods of dealing with life. Trolls, dwarves, elves, and other mystical beings may seem irrelevant but what they stand for isn't. They represent a link to a world that has become diminished by our electronic equipment. As we all know, technology has become the hub of society and rules our everyday lives. While this is an amazing truth, it can lead to society ignoring and damaging nature due to the development and use of electrical devices to run our lives.

Pagan is an umbrella term that covers nature-based beliefs, and it appeals to people who love the Earth and want to preserve it. It is growing in numbers in Europe and America because it appeals to people. The simple ways and links to the earth honor the world we live in and consider every being as equal. No misogyny, racism, judgment, or punishment is associated with paganism, and they include all forms of worship within their ranks. Imagine if that attitude spread, and we became a world that accepted everybody and every belief. Wouldn't that be amazing?

Magic in Medieval Times

Before Christianity appeared, magic was part of everyday life, and common folk would consult "witch doctors," "wise men," and other members of the community known as the "cunning folk" who influenced specific areas of their lives. They included the Tempestarii, a form of magi known for their influence over the weather. In periods of drought, they would perform rituals and spells to bring rain, and in times of floods, they would ask the gods for dry weather. The significance of their influence cannot be underestimated. The weather decided if the community would eat or starve as their crops were the staple part of their food chain.

Various spells and ointments would be procured to cure ailments that plagued the community. The locals would seek help for the lifting of curses and bring good luck when needed. These practices were only described as witchcraft with the arrival of Christian dominance in Europe. Pope Innocent III deemed pagan ways as devil-worshipping and evil and created a society that hunted down heretics and punished them. Some groups fled to Germany and the Savoy to escape his campaign to abolish their religion, and this became the home of the Cathars and other pagan groups.

As the growth of Christianity continued, the leading theologians of the era decided to demonize these groups, and they spread stories that Cathars and their followers were conducting devil-worshipping rituals filled with sex and evil deity connections. Further edicts from the Church described a world filled with evil demons and dangerous forces that were dedicated to tempting God-fearing Christians from the path of righteousness with promises of sex and debauched rituals. This began the long association of paganism and sex within the Christian faith.

This was not fun for pagans, and the Church was determined to rid the world of witchcraft and demon worship. They trained secular individuals to use any methods they could to force pagans to confess to their ill doings and witchery. This started a period known as the Inquisition, which resulted in the persecution of people who didn't follow Christian beliefs. It was the time of the "witch trials" and barbaric torture that the new orthodox rulings favored. Magic became a word synonymous with evil, and it has taken centuries for that to change.

Luckily, we are a more tolerant society now, and magic is encouraged and welcomed. We will look back at magical practices and explain how they can be used today to help us live better lives.

Chapter 2: The Cyprianus Tradition

Magic has been around for generations and has evolved because it has been passed down through the ages. These texts and manuscripts are often referred to as grimoires, but in Swedish magic, there is a more menacing term to cover spells and traditions collected through the ages. The Cyprianus texts don't apply to a standard text but are a general term used to cover the collection of spells and works that are indigenous to the Nordic area.

These manuscripts were sought out by common folk and ministers to learn how to summon magic beings and demons, but most forms of the black book were kept by the "cunning folk," the term used for folk healers and wise people who were often the older members of the community who were responsible for healing and thwarting evil. The books became part of folklore, and the owners could only pass them on to their descendants. They were impossible to get rid of in other ways and were impervious to being burned or destroyed by water.

The author was a bishop and martyr who lived in the early times of Christianity and was a sorcerer before his conversion. He attempted to bewitch a female saint but was overcome with faith when she made the sign of the cross above his head. This freed him from his devilish ties and converted him to Christianity. This description of Cyprianus originated in England in the 17th century and bore little resemblance to the Swedish tales of Cyprianus.

The Swedes believe he was an evil figure who originated from Norway and was a close consort of the Devil. One tale speaks of his deeds being so heinous that the Devil threw him out of hell. Cyprianus then exacted his revenge by writing the Cyprianus texts to share his depraved secrets with anyone who wanted to practice them.

In Denmark, the tale of Cyprianus is completely different. Their folklore tells of a Mexican nun who lived a chaste and pious life before the Devil noticed her good work. He captured the nun and cast her into a dungeon in the mid-14th century, where she was so distressed that she ripped off her habit and undergarments and wrote her magic knowledge on the cloth. These texts were found in the castle after her death.

Whatever name you prefer, the truth is that this is a book that needs to be handled with care. It is filled with spells and powerful incantations to summon the devil and give the user immense magical powers. A cautionary tale from German folklore tells the tale of a Russian soldier who faced a bevy of demons when he began to read his comrade's copy of the Cyprianus texts.

The Soldiers Tale

While seated by a fire, a Russian soldier inadvertently began to read the text his friend had left lying on the ground. A host of menacing demons immediately appeared and demanded that the soldier set them a task. Luckily the soldier knew that the only way to get rid of the demons was to set them a task they couldn't fulfill, so he told them to fill all the baths in the town with water that is transported using a sieve. After just a minute, the demons returned and told the soldier they had completed the task.

They demanded he set them another, and he told them to go to the Governor of the town and take down his house brick by brick without the knowledge of the inhabitants and then rebuild it in the same design. After just a minute, the demons returned, told him they had finished the deed and demanded another.

The soldier was bemused but thought he had a task they couldn't complete when he told them to visit the Volga River and count every grain of sand, every fish and how many droplets of water the river contained from its source to the mouth. They flew away but quickly returned with the answers he demanded. The soldier was at a loss to think of another task, and the demons were getting restless and threatened him with death if he didn't set them another task soon.

The soldier realized the spirits wouldn't come near him when he had the book in his hands. He picked the book up and began to read it, but the spirits increased and began to press him to act. He thought that if reading the book attracted the spirits, what would happen if he read it backward? He proceeded to read it from the end to the beginning, and he soon noticed that the spirits were fading and leaving the area. As he read on, they disappeared until he was left alone with the book. When his comrade returned, the soldier told him what had happened, and his comrade congratulated him on his actions. He confirmed that if he had continued to read traditionally, the demons would have consumed him on the stroke of midnight.

The spells are a mixed bag of folk remedies, incantations, and prayers with magical connections. They are as simple as healing a sprain or performing divination. Because the text is so diverse, the spells included are a fascinating collection of Nordic magic beliefs and practices.

To Heal a Sprained Foot

The incantation contains a poem about Jesus and his journey over the rocky ground on his horse. The horse stumbled and twisted its leg, and Jesus dismounted and healed the injury with his healing hands, praying to God. The spell suggests that the reader does the same and puts his faith in God, Jesus, and the Holy Ghost.

A Spell to Cast a Curse

A Scandinavian ritual for casting a curse onto an enemy involves a piece of paper, a pen, and a small box. The spellcaster writes the person's name to be cursed on the paper and then recites an incantation over the paper. This should include any personal details and the reason for the casting of the curse. Include what the curse should be, for example, bad luck, illness, or for their relationship to fail, before sealing the paper in the box. Take the box to a well or dig a hole in the garden. Put the box in the hole or cast it into the well while repeating the incantation you used when writing the person's name. Walk away and wait for the results.

How to Lift a Curse

Are you constantly getting dumped in relationships? Have you lost your job for no discernible reason? Are you constantly fighting illness or weight fluctuations? Maybe you have a hex or curse placed on you. If you think that someone has set a hex on you, follow the spell below to remove it:

What You Need to Do Is:
- Take a piece of strong paper or wax parchment and write down what you know about the hex. Who may have cast it? How has it affected your life? Include as much detail as you can.
- Add three tsp. of Himalayan salt
- Fold the paper until it forms a bundle. Tie the end with a string
- Make the bundle into a pendant and wear it around your neck for three days
- On the fourth day, untie the bundle and sprinkle the salt into running water, especially from natural sources like a river or the rain
- Burn the paper and string and bury the ashes
- Now, wear a crystal around your neck for nine days to heal the damage to your system the hex may have caused

Congratulations, you are now hex and curse-free!

Success Spells

What is success? More money, a better job, or a healthy relationship? Success means something different to everyone, and these spells from the black books of Scandinavia will help you improve your life generally and raise your level of success significantly.

Create a Talisman to Wear

What You Need:
- A purple candle
- A green candle
- A personal sigil or talisman (you can use a cross, a crystal, a star, or a crescent symbol, whatever you feel speaks to you)
- A chain

Create a sacred space by cleansing with sage or blessed water, then place the two candles opposite each other. Light both the candles and stand in-between them with your sigil in your right hand. Lift the purple candle with your right hand and walk slowly toward the green candle.

Place the purple candle next to the green one and recite a phrase that states your intention. Something like "I embrace and welcome success and happiness into my life," then attach the chain to the sigil and swing it between the flames.

Stop swinging when you feel your talisman is fully loaded and let the candles burn down naturally. Bury the wax in the garden and bless the space with a prayer. Wear the talisman whenever you feel the need for extra luck and success. Remember to reload this energy monthly and increase the potency by using the full moon to create extra magic powers.

Luck Spell

If you are feeling down because things aren't going your way, don't worry. We can change all that with magic. This spell is a simple ritual using household goods. In the black book, many spells use ingredients that are simple to obtain because there weren't the resources available to practitioners that there are today. We only need to open our smartphones, and we can access all kinds of magical ingredients, but that wasn't true back then.

What You Need:

- Vinegar, apple cider, white wine, or classic will do
- A representation of yourself, a picture, a personal piece of jewelry, or a lock of hair
- Two white candles
- Sea salt, Himalayan is best
- White dish

If you know the day you were born, then perform the spell on that day. If you don't, then perform it on Monday for added luck. Choose a time when you are alone and won't be disturbed.

Begin by placing the candles on a table or altar if you have one. Light them both and close your eyes. Stay still and silent for two minutes.

Bring your hands together and bow your head. Recite a phrase that speaks to your needs: "Bring me success and luck through the power of this ritual."

Place the representation of yourself on the white dish and wet it with the vinegar. Sprinkle salt on the vinegar and place the dish in front of the candles. Hold the candles until the wax drips on them, and then replace them on the table.

Blow out the candle and place your object in a dark space.

Wait for a week, and then take the object out of the dark. Take it with you wherever you go, and you'll be blessed with success and luck.

Love Spells

Witchcraft and trolldom are all about changing your life and making it better. Giving your love life a boost is a popular way to use spells and potions, so if you feel you are missing love and lust, try these spells adapted from the black book for modern times.

What You Need:
- Two candles, one white and one red
- Red ribbon
- Two pieces of paper and a pen
- Rose oil
- Red or pink cushion or cloth
- Fireproof dish or ashtray

Create a sacred space with a calm atmosphere and seat yourself on the cloth or cushion. Set up the two candles and join the bases with a red ribbon. Anoint the candles with the rose oil and write your name and the person you desire on the two pieces of paper.

Once the candles are lit, say your incantation. "I ask the universe for a union that will be loving and strong" or something that reflects your desires. Light both pieces of paper and let them burn in the fireproof dish. Let the candles burn down naturally, and then take the ashes outside and cast them into the wind.

Repeat the spell nine times for added strength and wait for the spell to attract the attention of your desired partner. The spell helps you feel open to love, increases your self-confidence, and enhances the magical forces of love.

How to Strengthen the Love Your Partner Has for You

Do you have a partner but feel the relationship is imbalanced? Do you want to turn up the heat in your relationship and make sure you both feel the same way? Try this powerful love spell to get things heated with your partner:

What You Need:
- Two red candles
- A silver chain
- Love spell oil with rosemary rose and vanilla essential oil
- Toothpick for carving

Create your sacred space and perform the spell when the new moon is in the sky. Take the toothpick and carve your name in one candle and your partner's name in the other. Wrap the silver chain around them and place them on a table or altar. Light them while reciting this incantation or one you have made up yourself, "This spell will call your heart to join mine in the realm of love. As these candles burn, we clear the way for love to blossom and grow."

Attract a Lost Love Back into Your Life

Why did you break up with someone you still love? If one of you cheated or significant issues caused the breakup, then walk away. This spell is designed to help when you have split with someone for reasons that seemed important at the time but are ridiculous. If insecurities and arguments drove you apart, try this healing spell to make the negative energies disappear:

What You Need:
- Two large white candles
- A purple candle
- Peppermint oil
- Sage for burning
- Rose incense stick

Cleanse the space with a sage smudge and then sit in the space while meditating. Remember all the enjoyable times you had with your partner and the laughs and love you shared. Now picture your future. The two of you are growing old and having a family or traveling the world. See yourself and your partner aging and loving each other through the future times.

Take the two white candles and name them, one with your name and the other with your ex-partner. Sprinkle peppermint oil on the candles and then light them, saying, "This candle is my Divine essence," and then the other saying, "This candle is (insert name of ex-partner" their Divine essence."

Light the purple candle, place it in front of the two white candles, and let it burn cleanly. Close your eyes and imagine the future once more filled with love and harmony. Now picture the conflicts you had disappearing with the smoke from the purple candle. Say something like, "We didn't know our love would suffer. We meant no harm. Let it be." Blow out all the candles and leave the space.

Witchcraft Tips for Beginners

The black book may be dedicated to Scandinavian magic from centuries ago, but the issues it deals with are just as relevant today. Love, luck, and success are important, and sometimes you must cast a hex to get revenge. The main thing to remember is to do no actual harm. If you do, you may experience the power of a three-fold return. This means that if you wish harm to someone, it will be returned to you three times over.

Use magic to do good things and bring positivity to your life. Follow these simple rules to make your witchcraft safe and effective.

- **Learn from various sources**. Witchcraft is subjective and should reflect your beliefs, so don't follow instructions rigidly. Take the teachings of others and make them personal. Beginners can be wary about straying from the path regarding spells, but if you are careful and respect the craft, you'll be fine.

- **Write down your experiences**. The black book or the Cyprianus tradition is the perfect example of why written records are so important. Without records, witchcraft would have died out generations ago. Create a Book of Shadows or your own grimoire to record your progress and note your growth.

- **Leave the fear behind**. Don't let fear hold you back; remember why you are doing your magic. How did you feel when you first started thinking about magic? Excited and filled with wonder? Become experiential and practice your craft regularly, so you become more masterful, and it becomes part of your everyday life.

- **Experiment with the craft.** Try new tools and practices that appeal to your personality. Witchcraft is all about embracing nature and trying innovative ideas. As you experiment, you'll be drawn to certain parts of the craft, let that natural attraction influence your choices, and go with the flow. Your inner self is very rarely wrong, so trust your gut and let yourself experience new techniques.

- **Don't worry about failure.** Not everything will work; failure is just part of the learning process. Don't be put off by spells that don't work. Try alternative ingredients and techniques. Practice makes perfect; even the most seasoned witches don't know everything and can get it wrong.

- **Don't overspend on tools and altars.** When you see popular witches and practitioners on social media, they will often be surrounded by ornate altars and collections of paraphernalia. It is easy to become overawed and rush out to buy loads of stuff but remember, you have all the time in the world to build your collection. Homemade tools and wands are often more powerful and effective than shop-bought items so take your time and only buy things you feel drawn to.

- **Join communities.** There are lots of groups and online communities to choose from, and this doesn't mean joining a coven. If being part of a coven makes you nervous, then start with like-minded groups that practice Wicca or other pagan and heathen practices. It takes time to become accustomed to talking freely about witchcraft, so choose a group you feel comfortable with. Stay safe and check out the resources before you give any details online and in person.

- **Accept the change.** Witchcraft and magic will change your life, and that is a fact. Don't be afraid. Nature and magic work together to connect you to the universe and improve your life. We are conditioned to believe that we aren't worthy of the better things in life, so you have to rise above those social dictates and accept your destiny.

- **Be culturally appropriate.** Some practitioners flaunt their beliefs and don't give a thought to other people. Not everyone believes, and that is their prerogative. It is also their right not to have witchcraft or paganism thrust into their lives. Don't force your ideas on other people, and don't wax lyrical about your new interest unless you are sure the other person is interested and won't be insulted or offended.

The black book is witchcraft from an age when it was normal to consult "crafty folk" to cure your ills. Modern practices can be adapted from these ancient ways to suit the life we lead today. Black magic has a bad reputation, but that was the fault of the early Christians. They were desperate to turn people away from paganism and make them believe it was evil. Most experts now recognize that the line between white and black magic is thin. Black magic is merely a different interpretation of white magic. If you are respectful and careful, it will work for you.

Chapter 3: The Power of Herb Magic

Herbs are a staple part of our kitchens and are readily available. They have been used for generations as healing ingredients and home remedies. Most modern medicines seek to cure symptoms and rely on stronger drugs to deal with the causes of illness and underlying issues. Of course, modern medicine shouldn't be cast aside, but the ideal way to use herbology is to use it in conjunction with regular medicines to create a healthier way of treating ailments.

Humans are complicated organisms that are subject to attack by forces that mean to harm us. Germs, viruses, and other harmful forces need to be repelled, and we need to keep our bodies in a healthy form to combat the dangers we face daily. Herbology is the study of combining natural ingredients to form a strong defense against these forces and make us more stable and immune to their harmful properties.

Herbology is a magical way to keep yourself safe and feel better. Remember those special teas or hot drinks that your grandma made to make you feel special when you had a cold? Maybe a family recipe for a special soup when you were ill? Chances are that the herbs included in them were added by someone who knew their herbal magic and how to combine them to make a magical remedy passed down through the family for generations.

In this next section, we will uncover the properties that herbs bring to magic and when they should be used. Three specific types of magic are covered, and a list of herbs can increase the potency of your spells and remedies.

Protection Spells

Acacia

Also known as Wattle or Mimosa, this herb grows in warm climates and is partly used to anoint sacred spaces and create healing baths. The young leaves and flowers are edible and can be used in teas and potions. Use this herb to break hexes and curses and consecrate your magic tools.

African Violet

Violets can be found growing everywhere and are a great ingredient for making teas and syrups, but African violets can cause indigestion and should be used solely to protect the home when burned as incense. Use it to power your amulets and wear them around your neck.

Alder

This herb is found in trees growing near the riverbanks and is harvested by collecting the catkins that hang from the branches. The herb is filled with protein and astringent and can be used as a strong anti-inflammatory ingredient. Use in potions to create weather magick and influence decision-making. The herb is associated with the protection of the newly deceased and is often used in teas at funerals.

Aloe Vera

This plant grows wild in tropical and arid places but can be purchased in many forms from suitable sources. It has been used for medicinal purposes for over 6,000 years and is a handy part of your magical life. Add the leaves to salads or use the gel to enhance teas or as a dressing for dips. Water containing aloe can be bought from your supermarket, which will help you balance your body heat when the temperatures soar.

Althea Root

This powerful herb grows near lakes and marshes and is also known as marshmallow root. It can be consumed raw to aid coughs and colds or can be steeped in water to create a tea that cures dry mouth and protects against ulcers. It can be used as a poultice to treat burns and wounds or soothe skin irritation.

Angelica

This decorative hardy herb is found in colder climates and has multiple healing properties. It protects the body from toxins and increases blood circulation. It has been used for centuries to treat menstruation problems and is often called female ginseng. It is believed the name originates from the tale of a monk who received the herb from the heavens to help him treat people suffering from the plague. Use it to flavor foods and drinks with a smoky musky taste and aroma for daily use.

Basil

Basil
https://pixabay.com/images/id-1248955/

This common herb can be grown everywhere, and even the smallest pot will yield a healthy amount. Use it to drive away hostile spirits and sprinkle it in your bath for a magical protective shield. Add it to the final cooking stage to keep the herb fresh and effective. In Europe, basil is used to create holy water utilized in the church due to its strong protective qualities.

Bergamot

Wild bergamot is found in North America and is used in gardens to attract butterflies and bees to the area. It reduces cholesterol and relieves stress. Use the herb in its natural form or use the essential oil to flavor teas and potions. Add to your remedies to alleviate joint pain and increase mental alertness. Bergamot oil used in aromatherapy is a powerful way to relieve anxiety and protect the user from stress.

Black Cohosh

A Woodland herb native to North America, black cohosh is used to alleviate women's estrogen-related symptoms like night sweats, hot flashes, and other menopausal and menstrual conditions. It also relieves headaches and is a powerful aid in improving digestion function. Use it in teas or potions, or take it as a capsule.

Black Pepper

This common household condiment is also a powerful magic ingredient. Mix it with salt to scatter around the home for protection or to season your food. Burn black pepper for a powerful smudge or use it as incense to clear the home from negative energies.

Boneset

Grown in North America, this is a lesser-known herb of the magnoliids family of plants. It has been used for generations by Native North Americans to treat respiratory conditions and ease fevers. Mix with peppermint leaves and elder herb to make a tea to guard against allergies, viruses, and colds. It will strengthen your immunity and make your bones stronger.

Burdock

Grown in Europe and Asia, this herb is a powerhouse of antioxidants and removes toxins from the blood. It is rich in fiber and helps regulate blood pressure and digestion. The natural properties of burdock help the liver function well and promote flawless skin. It can be added to food and drink in dried form, or the roots can be eaten raw.

Calamint

Found growing in the temperate regions of Europe, calamint clears any airway infections and stops digestive cramps and convulsions. It is an effective congestion relief, and you can use the flowers, stems, and leaves depending on your needs. Use in tea or to flavor foods.

Caraway

This herb is found in Asia, Europe, and Africa and is a relative of the carrot. In ancient times herbalists used the seeds to relieve digestive gas and as a general tonic for digestion.

Catnip

This aromatic herb is found in central Europe and has been used in food preparation for generations. Its leaves are great for herbal teas, and the herb is also added to tonic wines and liquor. Mix the leaves with your salad for a tasty protective way to aid sleep or create a calming effect on the nerves.

Chia

One of the more modern "superfoods," chia seeds, have been used in herbology for generations. Eat them in a salad for nutrition, or use their magical properties to protect yourself from gossip and slander.

Chives

Another common herb that has strong protective properties. It was used in exorcisms and banishing to keep the subject safe from evil. Use these properties and add chives to your diet and your magic potions.

Cinquefoil

This herb is prolific in Europe and grows easily in most gardens. Use it to treat swellings in the mouth and blisters or ulcers. It is a powerful laxative and, as a tea, it is used to treat colds and flu by reducing inflammation. Used externally, it can reduce the pain of insect stings, wounds, and acne. Crush the roots and flowers, add them to a jar of vodka and leave them in a dark space for ten days. Filter the liquid through a cloth and use it as a daily supplement to strengthen your immune system. This potion is more potent than the tea, so a teaspoon a day will suffice.

Cloves

Sourced from Asia and South America, cloves will help you dispel negativity and stop gossip. They are an effective pain relief method and have been used to ease toothache for thousands of years. Add to meat dishes and curries to promote health and protection for your immune system.

Comfrey

This is a prolific herb and can be found in most environments. It is effective in curing skin issues and is also used as a muscle relaxant. Its magical uses include travel protection; a sachet in your luggage will protect you from theft and other issues.

Devils Bit

This ingredient is a rare herb from Europe that can bring love and protection and increase your chances of romance. Use it as a tea or as a tincture to treat bruises and wounds. Traditional folklore says that the plant's appearance looks like the head has been bitten off because the Devil was so jealous of the plant's magical properties that he wanted to deprive humankind of its virtues.

Devils Claw

Native to South America this herb resembles a gnarled hook-like hand which led to its rather ominous name. It is used to treat gout and other inflammatory issues, and, in magic, it is a powerful protection ingredient. Hang sachets around your home to keep you safe from evil spirits.

Dogwood

This herb is an intensely powerful way to guard your journals. Use it to protect your book of shadows or grimoires.

Elder

Elder is a prolific plant found in most climates and is the source of the elder herb, which is especially effective when treating colds and flu. In potions, it helps protect from viral infections and makes the immune system stronger. Ground elder can help cure gout and other joint pain.

Eucalyptus

This herb is sourced from Australia and Tasmania and includes over five hundred species of plants. It can be used topically to treat acne and skin complaints and provides a healing balm for burns and other wounds. Inhaling the oil helps respiratory issues and promotes relaxation. The plant should never be consumed fresh, but the dried leaves can be used in tea to decrease blood pressure and relieve anxiety and stress. Its eucalyptol oil is a natural insect repellant and can be used to keep your home bug free.

Fennel

Originally from Europe, this hardy perennial herb can now be found worldwide. It is a member of the carrot family and is full of flavor. The seeds can be added to potions to provide anti-bacterial properties and nutrition. The seeds can be used to make a tea that helps relieve anemia, constipation, and wind. They are also delicious when roasted and served as a side dish.

Figwort

Found throughout the Northern hemisphere, figwort has been used in herbal medicine for generations and is a powerful part of your herb collection. Hundreds of different species are used to treat skin conditions like psoriasis and eczema. It can be added to potions to stimulate the heart and acts as a laxative. If you have a heart condition, avoid this herb as it can make it worse and affect the rhythm of your heart.

Fleabane

A common medicinal wildflower, this handy plant can be sued to treat urogenital diseases like gonorrhea and urinary tract infections. Its Mexican cousin can be used to treat toothache and other oral issues. In magic potions, it is a source of protection against negative energy and is used in exorcisms.

Galangal

A member of the ginger family, galangal is found in Asia and is a staple part of Thai cuisine. In traditional medicinal practices, it is used to treat dysentery, skin conditions, and bad breath. It increases the sperm count and is used in potions to boost fertility.

Garlic

A staple part of most kitchen supplies, garlic is both practical and one of the more magical plants available. It famously repels vampires and is used to purify spaces and objects. Use it to protect your home and your sacred spaces and carry it when you feel exposed to other people's negativity.

Ginger

Another common part of your kitchen supplies is adding ginger to your potions to bring good health and protection. Dried ginger can be added to mojo bags for extra magical potency.

Ginseng

Found in South China, ginseng varieties are now available in the USA and can be used in magic to promote sexual potency and performance. It helps memory and promotes magical connections by improving cognitive forces. Medicinally it also reduces the metabolism and boosts the cells to fight infections.

Heather

Traditionally used by Romany people to bring good luck and fortune, heather is a common plant with magical properties. Burn a smudge stick of heather and fern to bring rain and hang it around the house to bring peace and harmony. Carry it on your person to protect yourself from attacks and sexual crimes.

Juniper

This magical berry is one of the oldest trees on earth. It is found on every continent and can survive the harshest climates and lack of water. It represents wisdom and perseverance and can promote raised vibrations and open your third chakra when used as a smudge. Carry the berries to protect you while you travel and use them in a bath to attract love and new relationships.

Lady Slipper

Found across the northern hemisphere, these hardy orchids are added to potions to promote sleep. It is quite expensive and should only be included in your herbal collection if you are experiencing difficulties with sleeping.

Lavender

Another common herb, it is said that burning lavender is a powerful way to promote restful auras. Burn the flowers and scatter the ashes to bring peace to your area.

Mandrake

Another traditional herb used for centuries, mandrake, is found in southern Europe and North Africa. Its roots look like human genitalia; they help the wearer attract new sexual partners when carried. Slip a mandrake root beneath your pillow to encourage fertility and conception. Mandrake oil is used to anoint candles to increase their potency.

Marigold

The common garden flower should be added to baths to bring confidence and protection while you sleep.

Marshmallow Root

This is a slippery root used for medicinal properties for generations. It soothes inflammation, and in potions, it helps to cure colds and sore throats. It originates in Africa but can be found in herbal supply outlets worldwide. The Ancient Greeks used marshmallow root to create a balm for insect stings, while the Romans used it as a laxative.

Mint

Simple to grow and incredibly powerful, mint is a protective herb that can be added to most dishes and teas to create a tasty magical force.

Nutmeg

Another kitchen staple sprinkles it on green candles in spells for money or prosperity. It gives the wearer protection when used to make amulets or added to mojo bags.

Orris Root

This hybrid plant is used in perfumes and scents but in magic; it is better known for its drawing power. It can draw toxins out both physically and spiritually and is also used to promote dreamwork and divination powers. It has powerful connections to the female arts and is used as an attraction herb in rituals concerning passion and romance. Medicinally, it boosts the nervous system and is also effective in oral health.

Pimpernel

Part of the burnet plant family, this brilliant scarlet flower grows wild and can be harvested easily. It has a reputation for its supposed narcotic quality, but wild pimpernel won't contain anything that will alter your state of mind. The dried leaves brewed in a tea will provide a carminative relief for wind and aid any other digestive issues.

Red Clover

Originally sourced in Europe, the plant has been naturalized in most regions and can be found in most countries. It is used to treat skin conditions and menstruation ailments and to purify the liver and digestive tract. In magic, it is also used to purify areas, especially when used in a smudge. Red clover tea helps stimulate the brain and reduces anxiety, and adding mint and hibiscus brings added wisdom.

Rowan

Known as the sacred witch tree, rowan has featured in magical rituals and practices since the time of the druids. In Norse mythology, the first woman was crafted from the bark of the rowan, and it is the preferred wood for creating magical talismans and runes. They are planted in graveyards to protect the dead, and their berries are used in protection spells. They contain slightly toxic acids, so they must be cooked before they are ready to digest.

Rue

Found in the Mediterranean, this herb is known as the queen of herbs. It is used in magic to protect the users from evil and lift curses and hexes. It is added to potions that are used for purification and can be added to baths for spiritual cleansing. It is used in lovers' incense when mixed with sandalwood and lavender.

Sandalwood

Another common herb should be scattered around the home to protect and purify the space. It is used in exorcism rituals and will help you banish negativity and evil.

Spearmint
Use spearmint leaves or oil in a bath for strength, vitality, and protection.

St. John's Wort
This prolific wildflower has been used in magic since the Middle Ages to protect households from evil spirits and witches. Today we know it is a healthy way to lift the spirits and ease addictive tendencies. Use it in house purifications or potions to keep the body healthy and rested.

Thistle
The common thistle is prickly and can cause skin irritation. Use it carefully to make tea for protection or hang it in the house to ward off negativity.

Witch Hazel
Found in North America, Japan, and China, this plant is a strong astringent and can be used to clean wounds and calm stings. Wiccan spells include witch hazel to create an emotional balance and purge the mind of troubling energy.

These herbs and plants give you a base to work with since we always need protection when performing witchcraft. Other elements are added to give meaning to potions and spells to create a mixture of magical properties to enhance your knowledge.

These individual herbs will signal your intent and bring strength and power to your work:

Love, Passion, Sex, and Romance

Adam and Eve's Roots
Native to North America, these roots come in different shapes that resemble male and female genitalia. In traditional spells, the male will take the female root, and the female will take the male root to attract members of the other sex. Of course, modern magic works just as well in same-sex and polygamous relationships so just adapt the ritual to the needs of the people involved. Carry both roots in a magic bag to attract a proposal or new love.

Black Cohosh

This common plant yields natural elements to help sleep and fertility. It can be bought dried from herbal resources and used to make tea and boost your chances of attracting love.

Caraway

These seeds are often found in cakes, but in magic, they are used to bind lovers to you and stop them from straying or cheating.

Cardamon

Sourced in India and the subcontinents, this tasty herb is used in curries and other spicy dishes. In magic, it is a powerful ingredient in love and lust magic. Placed in a pouch with other Venus-related objects, it will attract love and passion.

Chamomile

Use a restful bath to prepare yourself for new love and increased potency.

Chili Pepper

Also known as cayenne, this is another staple direct from your kitchen cupboard. This spicy herb is a sure-fire ingredient that adds heat to your love life and breaks hexes. Add it to your foods or use it in your potions to add spice and get your love muscles flexing.

Elecampane

Part of the sunflower family, it is native to Eurasia and is a powerful plant when performing magic to attract love. It was used in Ancient Greece as a tonic that enriched the blood and helped the heart function healthily.

Evening Primrose

Native Americans have used this North American wildflower for generations for performing magic. Use it in a bath to reveal your inner beauty or in spells that promote success and achieve your goals. Because it flowers at night, it works well with spells relating to moon magic and the goddess Diana.

Laurel

Native to Asia Minor, use this herb to decorate your altar, enhance psychic dreams, and reveal the name of your next true love. To keep a current love true, both of you should visit a laurel tree, choose a leaf, and split it in two. If you both keep hold of your half of the leaf, neither of you will be tempted to stray.

Lovage

Use in a bath to enhance your natural attractiveness and draw potential partners to your energy.

Marjoram

Another staple kitchen herb, just adding a few leaves will enhance any love spell, or you can just put it in your food.

Myrtle

One of the most powerful love herbs in your collection, it has been used for generations to decorate crowns for grooms and brides and to decorate marriage altars. It was reputedly the name used for women's genitalia back in Ancient Greece. Use it fresh or as an oil to boost love spells for intimacy and to strengthen connections.

Parsley

This kitchen staple can be worn in your shoe to make you more attractive to others.

Periwinkle

Grown in Madagascar, this pretty flower is essential in love spells and potions. Burn the dried leaves before having sex with your partner to intensify the experience.

Quassia

Originating in South America, this is a healthy herb used in herbal medicine, but in magic, it can ensure you keep your relationship. Simply take a lock of your hair and add one from your lover, burn the hair on some quassia chips and then keep the ashes safe to preserve the love you have for each other.

Saffron

This expensive and glorious spice can be used to make the blandest dish look and taste amazing. In magic, just a nip of saffron will do the same for your potions and spells, especially when you are conjuring passion and love.

Sesame

Another common herb adds to your spells to attract lust and success.

Tonka Beans

A popular ingredient in Hoodoo magic, Tonia beans are used to attract love and passion.

Ylang Ylang

Use the essential oil to enhance your sexual spells and bring the power of fairy magic to your work.

Abundance Spells

Basil

Used to create new opportunities for financial success. Add to your spells for abundance, and when you cleanse your sacred space, add basil leaves to the hot water for prosperity.

Comfrey

This magic herb is commonly found in the wild and is often used to treat skin conditions. It brings strength to spells regarding real estate or property in magical terms. Carry some with you when you travel to keep yourself and your belongings safe.

Fenugreek

Burn the dried leaves to attract money and fertility. Place in a jar with protection herbs and add a small amount every day. As the jar fills, so will your bank account.

Hollyhock

This impressive bush should be grown near your home to attract wealth and prosperity to you and the occupants.

Irish Moss

A species of red algae that grows on rocks around the Atlantic part of Europe, this is a handy ingredient in abundance spells.

Jobs Tears

Asiatic grass is used in magic to represent luck when finding employment and money. Use the grass in lucky bags and bring good luck to your spells.

Thyme

Add to your bath to bring luck, prosperity, and a constant flow of money to your home.

Obviously, this list is just a few herbs and plants available for your crafting. Like traditional cooking, whenever you find a new ingredient, you will be tempted to add it to your spells. Also, you'll find your individual favorites and special herbs and plants that you can add to any mixture to make it personal.

Herbology is a never-ending learning curve, but don't let that make you feel overwhelmed. It is fun, providing you do your research and avoid poisonous ingredients. Keep yourself safe and enjoy your herbal experiments.

Chapter 4: Cauldron Magic

The word cauldron conjures up an image of a gnarled old hag cackling as she stirs her potions in a large metal pot over an open flame. While this image may have been true centuries ago, most modern witches recognize the need to go with the times and use more modern pots to brew their potions. It is important to remember that whatever your cauldron or pot is made of could make it difficult to care for.

Cast iron pots can be a nightmare to keep clean even if they do look the part. Some herbs also react badly to iron, and this can make a potion go bad or even cause harm to the recipient. Fortunately, there are more modern materials that are more suited to potion brewing so let's look at the materials available depending on what your potions will be:

Cast Iron

Cast iron cauldrons are traditionally used.
https://pixabay.com/images/id-3818908/

The traditional pots look great and make your spells feel more authentic, and are great if you use them just for burning incense or herbs for cleansing purposes. You can buy a relatively inexpensive model from online resources or search thrift shops for a more traditional iron pot. Dutch ovens are another way to convert modern cooking utensils into a tool for witchcraft and are easily sourced. Remember that cleaning your cauldron is essential, and iron models can be more labor-intensive.

Ceramic

Cauldrons made from ceramics can be beautiful, lighter to use, and easier to clean. They look great on your kitchen shelves, and you can buy them with personal decorations to make your work more personalized. Ceramic models are generally less expensive than metal pots, and you can buy them easily from most retail sources. Don't forget that ceramic pots come in all shapes and sizes, and even a teacup can be used for smaller potions or burning incense. True witches care more about the end result than their tools' aesthetics.

Glass

This is a controversial material for some witches, but many more are beginning to appreciate the aesthetic value of glass cauldrons. The sheer wonder of watching your potion brew from all angles has persuaded even the most traditional witches to use them for their potions. Make sure the glass is heat-proof and the pot is fairly robust. Some glass pots are only meant for decoration and won't withstand more vigorous stirring or being heated and cooled.

When you choose a cauldron, remember to choose one with a lid if needed and a handle if you plan to take your magic with you on your travels. Don't use your cauldron for everyday cooking, as you risk contamination and lowering your work's magical properties. Like your other tools, the cauldron is an extension of you and shouldn't be used by others. It isn't part of your household goods and should be kept for special occasions.

What Are Potions?

Quite simply, a potion is a liquid made with magical intentions. It can be used as a drink or for topical use. It can also be used to bless items and cleanse both physical and spiritual areas. They can also be referred to as elixirs, infusions, balms, or magical balms. No matter what you call it, the power of potions is a combination of the ingredients combined and the ritual of preparation.

How to Start Your Potion

Remember that just like a regular cooking area, the space you are using needs to be clean, but even more so in the process of magic potions. The area you are using should be physically clean and spiritually free from debris. Create a cleansing smoke by burning sage or your favorite herb and pass all your ingredients and tools through the smoke to cleanse them. Take the burning sage to the four points of the room and say a few healing words to make the effect more intense. Banish negative energy and make the space feel grounded and sacred.

Magic Potion-Based Liquids

When you start creating potions, knowing where to start can be daunting, so beginners and experts recognize the importance of a base liquid. Witches often avoid potions because they seem complicated and can easily go wrong. Think of creating portions the same way you approach your ordinary cooking skills, which involve a recipe that can be adjusted to suit your needs. How many times have you taken a well-loved recipe and made it your own? The same principle applies to magic. Once the basics are covered, you can change the potions to suit you and your magic.

Choose a Base Liquid

When making a potion, choosing the base liquid that suits the spell you are creating is important. Here is a list of some basic liquids that work well with herbs, crystals, and other magic ingredients.

- **Water:** Perhaps the most accessible source of liquid but also the most versatile. Tap water works, but where's the imagination in that? Try infusing your water with crystals or leaving it in the moon's light to become "moon water" or infusing it with sunlight. Try natural sources to bring the power of nature to your spells and use river or spring water. If your spell involves traveling, then use seawater to bring in the power of nature's mighty oceans. Remember to use filtered or bottled water if your spell is going to be consumed.

- **Fruit or Vegetable Juice:** Who says you can't have healthy potions? Use bright-colored juices to add a splash of flavor and vitamins to your potions. The magical properties of the colors and the magical quality of the place where it was grown could be used.

- **Red, White, or Rose Wine:** When you use alcohol, you need to be careful if you share your potion but if it is for your own use, then go for it. Wine is a great base for potions and works well with herbs and other natural ingredients. Remember, if you're heating wine, the alcohol content will often be dissipated, and the liquid will lose its potency.

- **Natural Sources:** If you can drink it, you can use it in a potion, providing it isn't too processed. If you are creating a potion that will be drunk, then your base can also be a drinkable liquid like tea or coffee. There are so many natural alternatives you can use, like plant-based milk or yogurt, that the choices are both endless and healthy.

- **Oils:** Oils make the perfect base if your potion is for topical use. Almond or other nut oils are easily purchased from local sources, making a smoother and easy-to-apply potion. While some oils can be expensive, plain vegetable oil is a cheaper alternative, readily found in most kitchen cupboards.

Now you have the basics. A clean area, your chosen cauldron, a glass jar to keep the finished product in, and your athame to chop the ingredients. You also need a heat source when cooking your potion and relative safety equipment when using a naked flame. Your ritual must speak to all four of the elements to invoke the power of nature, so the heat source is your connection to the fire, the base liquid is water, the steam is an air connection, and your ingredients are linked to the earth.

State your intentions as you prepare for your ritual. Thank the elements for their daily presence in your life. Ask the spirits to join you in your work and encompass their energy into what you are doing. Spells always work better with well-stated intentions, and potions are no different. Positive statements will put you in the right frame of mind and help you focus.

Magical Potions

Now you have the knowledge of herbs and plants and your cauldron, it is time to dive into the magical world of potions. This section will explore some simple beginners' potions and then progress to more complex mixtures. Throughout history, potions have been produced to cure all manner of ailments, from simple illness to finding love, securing immortality, or curing the plague. In the medieval ages, doctors and trained apothecaries were mostly male and required payment for their services, while those who couldn't afford to pay for their potions turned to local wise women to administer their homemade potions and salves, performing prayers and chants to increase their efficiency. These were early forms of witchcraft, and they were administered to members of society who were impoverished.

Scandinavians especially featured love potions known as Philters, which were documented in the Norse poem "The Lay of Gudrun" from the Poetic Edda. Norse mythology is filled with tales of potions, salves, elixirs, and other magical mixtures that influence others.

Here are some modern takes on trolldom and Norse potions. Feel free to add or change the recipes to suit your needs, ingredients, and intentions. Some of these potions are made from ingredients in your kitchen cupboards, while others will take more effort.

Self-Love Potion

The best way to make your work effective is to believe in it. The ingredients, the method, and most of all, the person doing it, yes, that's you, so making your first potion a self-love mixture makes perfect sense.

The Hibiscus Love Potion

This simple herbal tea has no caffeine content and can be consumed both heated and cold. Make a batch to keep in the fridge for when you need a boost of self-confidence.

What You Need:
- Hibiscus tea
- Sugar
- Mint leaves
- Pink candle
- Small metal container
- Cup
- Water

Dress your altar with a candle and a white cloth. Turn off all your electronics and keep them out of your sacred area. Play soothing music or just enjoy the silence. Heat the water in the metal container with the candle flame while you recite the following "I am loved, I am worthy of that love, and I accept it with the power of the universe. Bring me a wave of inner peace, and let me rid myself of negativity and darkness while I let the light of the world fill me up."

Add the tea and water to your cup and sweeten it to taste. Sprinkle the mint and drink after it has brewed. As you sip the tea, imagine your best life, that job you know you are worthy of, the partner you know you deserve, and see yourself surrounded by the love of people around you.

A Healing Potion for Low-Level Ailments or to Boost Energy

This is a simple brew that will make you feel energized and drive those nagging ailments away.

What You Need:

- 2 small pieces of willow bark
- 1 tbsp. vanilla extract
- 1 tbsp. apple juice
- A pinch of sage
- Pinch of rosemary
- 2 drops of lemon juice
- Water

Dress your altar with a light blue cloth and place the ingredients in your cauldron. Add your preferred base liquid. We have used water in this example and boiled the liquid. As the water boils, recite this mantra "Healing liquid be my balm, stop the pain and heal the harm." Once the liquid has cooled, pour it into a cup and sip the tea while imagining all the pain leaving your body. Imagine the white light filling you with energy and excitement for what the day holds for you, and picture the fatigue leaving your body and floating away into the ether.

Healing Potion Made with Ingredients from Your Kitchen

This potion is especially effective for colds, sore throats, laryngitis, and menstrual issues

Cold and Flu Potion

What You Need:

- Ginger, either dried or ground root
- 1 tbsp. lemon juice
- 1 tbsp. Manuka honey
- A pinch of cinnamon
- Brown sugar
- Water or lemon tea

This can be brewed on your altar or created in your kitchen on the stove. Add all the ingredients to a pot and let it simmer for ten minutes while you recite the following: "Magic potion, do your thing, clear my throat so I can sing, let your magic soothe my soul and make me feel whole forever." Once the potion has cooled, sweeten it and drink whenever needed.

Protection Potion to Keep Negative Energy at Bay

This potion can be ingested to keep you safe or used to sprinkle around your home for added protection. It can be bottled and used for up to three months after brewing.

What You Need:

- Jasmin tea bag
- 1 tbsp. Manuka honey
- 2 cloves
- 1 tbsp. lemon juice
- 3 bay leaves
- Sprinkle of black pepper

- Water
- Cup
- Sugar

Dress your altar in gold or red cloth and decorate with your favorite crystals or gemstones. Add anything you feel represents your favorite parts of your life, like your house keys, jewelry, or pictures of your family or friends.

Place the cauldron on the altar, add the ingredients (except the sugar), and repeat the following prayer. "I call upon the divine to make me feel safe. Bless me with your all-encompassing energy and shield me from harm. Be my guardian and give me the strength to shield others and myself."

Now take the cauldron to your kitchen and brew the potions. Use it to consecrate your home or drink it depending on your needs. Imagine a bright white dome surrounding all the things you love, and then picture the negative forces being repelled into the darkness.

Alcoholic Potions Just for Adults

Raspberry Honey Potion

This boozy potion is to cleanse and purify your energy and attract new love or friends

What You Need:
- Raspberry vodka
- Raspberry tea
- Hibiscus tea
- 1 tsp caramel syrup
- Lemon juice
- Honey
- Peppermint cordial
- Ice
- Cocktail shaker or cauldron

You can make the process more magical by dressing your altar in pink, yellow, or white cloths and a couple of candles, but this potion really is just about the end product. Add all the ingredients to your chosen receptacle and either stir or shake. Add the ice as you mix or put it into a glass to cool the liquid. As you sip your potion, thank the gods, goddesses, and the universe for your good fortune and thank them for their interest in you and your life.

A Love Potion Based on Wine

This is a tasty potion designed for long hot summer days filled with the promise of romance and the joy of new love

What You Need:

- Wine, you can use white or rose
- Fresh peaches
- Raspberries
- Vanilla pods
- Sprig of mint
- Ice
- Glass

Fill a glass with ice and add the wine. As you add the other ingredients, ask the heavens to send you positive energy and a vision of your perfect partner. Once the potion has been stirred and chilled, sip it slowly and imagine how the two of you will look in the future. Thank the goddess of love and romance for her help.

Alcohol-Based Sleep Potion

Take this warming potion before you go to bed; it will help you fall asleep and promote positive dreams. This comforting potion will make you feel drowsy and warm as you fall into a deep slumber.

What You Need:

- 1 shot of dark rum
- Cinnamon
- Dark sugar
- Water or milk, depending on your taste
- An orange candle

- Lavender essence
- Cauldron
- Cup

Dress your altar with muted color cloth and place the orange candle on the surface. Put the rum, cinnamon, sugar, and water/milk in your cauldron on the stove and bring it to a boil before letting it simmer for two minutes. Bring the cauldron to the altar, light the candle, and sprinkle the essence on your altar as you pour the potion into a cup. Recite the following "Take me to the land of rest and let my sleep be the best, help me dream of past and present, and show me how to be ready for the future."

Drink the potion and let your eyes droop as you imagine the future filled with love and success.

Wine-Based Potion for Love and Lust

This sexy potion will bring a romantic boost to even the most tired love life. Make a cauldron full and keep it bottled for when you want a repeat session with your loved one.

What You Need:
- A bottle of sweet red or white wine
- 5 fresh basil leaves
- 6 red rose petals
- 3 cloves
- 4 apple seeds
- 2 drops of pomegranate essence
- 2 oz. raspberry juice
- A large piece of ginseng root
- Cauldron
- Tea cloth for straining
- Glass jar with a sealable top

Decorate your altar with red and white cloths, and then add white quartz, moonstone, and garnet to the table. Add all the ingredients to the cauldron and take it to the kitchen. Decorate the area you are working in with colored candles and tea lights. Stir the mixture over low heat and say,

"I give this wine to show my love and hope they find it tasty, bring my love into my life and make their arrival hasty." As it cools, thank the goddess of love Freya for her ministrations and then bottle it. Keep it in the fridge until you find the person you feel is worthy of your love.

Other Regular Potions for Everyday Life

Strictly speaking, coffee and other daily beverages are not tied to Norse traditions but are part of modern Scandi and Nordic life today. Adapt your potions and rituals to include them, so you don't miss a trick when it comes to introducing magic into your routine.

Daily Coffee Potion

Have you ever thought of the magical properties of coffee? In the olden days, it was referred to as "Satan's brew," so its ties with magic go back further than you think. What do you feel when you have coffee? Happier, energized, comforted, or inspired? Coffee has multiple uses apart from being a drink. It energizes our system and boosts energy so remember to treat the humble java with the respect it deserves and keep it in your kitchen store.

Use Brewed Coffee for These Magical Uses

- Remove blockages by sipping the liquid or bathing in it. Add some herbs or essential oils to a bath to remove negativity from your aura and your environment.
- Remove a curse by using coffee as a base liquid for a protection spell, or drink it while you repeat the source of the curse to ensure you dispel the energy behind the hex.
- Dispel negative spirits by washing your sacred space with a diluted solution of coffee and sage.
- Improve your luck by stirring the coffee vigorously to create bubbles and then using a spoon to scoop them up and drink.
- Connect with the deities by offering them a tasty cappuccino or espresso. They are just as fond of their brew as you are and will be pleased to share your daily routine.

Money Potion

Use this potion to attract wealth and financial success and improve any business you conduct. The potion can be drunk cold or hot and stored in a jar for up to a week.

What You Need:
- 4 cups of water
- 2 sticks of cinnamon
- 4 cloves
- 1 tsp all spice powder
- 2 sprigs of fresh mint
- 2 tsp. brown sugar

Dress your altar in green and gold cloth and light a white candle anointed with your favorite oil. Place three-dollar bills on the altar. Take your cauldron to the kitchen and boil the water and all the other ingredients except the fresh mint for five minutes. Cover the cauldron and let the mixture steep for ten minutes off the heat. Repeat the following "Money and cash are nice to own; they make me happy and fill my soul if the universe wills it to bring that wealth and love to me."

Take the liquid and add the fresh mint. Leave it to cool before straining it and serving it with ice or as a reheated beverage. Feel the emotion you will experience as you receive your rewards while you sip the potion. After you have finished, thank the spirits for their help. For further strength, sprinkle the potion on the dollar bills and leave them on your altar.

Increased Focus Potion

Feeling a bit stressed and experiencing low energy levels? Are you struggling to focus on work or at home, or do you just want to empower your mind? Try this refreshing potion to bring energy to your aura and elevate your senses.

What You Need:
- 6 fresh lemons
- 4 cups of water
- A sprig of fresh rosemary

- Brown sugar
- Honey
- Lime juice
- Bay leaves
- Glass
- Ice

Make the basic juice by squeezing the lemons into three cups of water. As you squeeze, empower them by visualizing a smarter and sharper you after you have taken the potion. Imagine those awesome ideas you'll have and the positivity flowing from your mind. Set the juice aside to infuse with the rest of the ingredients.

On the stove, heat the remaining water with the rosemary, sugar, and honey. Let it boil for ten minutes until all the sugar has dissolved. Now let the mixture cool as you imagine the success you'll find in the future. That new job or the prospect of new experiences, let your senses become laser-focused on your future.

Add ice to a glass and pour in the lemon liquid. Remove the rosemary sprig and use the sweet liquid to enchant the lemony taste. Create a sweet elixir to promote your mental health and enjoy.

Aphrodisiac Passion Potion

This potion is a powerful way to warm someone up and get them in the mood for love, but they are not miracle mixtures. They will not make someone who has no interest in you change their mind, but they will bring passion back to a relationship that may have gone flat.

Bring the Heat Potion

What You Need:
- Sprig of rosemary
- ½ tsp thyme
- A pinch of sage
- A pinch of nutmeg
- 2 tsp mint tea leaves
- 3 cloves

- 3 rose petals
- 6 drops of lemon juice
- Water
- Picture of your loved one
- A piece of rose quartz

Set up your altar with red and pink cloths and light three white candles. Set the picture and the quartz in front of the middle white candles. Add the other ingredients to your cauldron and heat them over the candles, or take them into the kitchen and warm them on the stove.

As the mixture cools, repeat the following "Love and heat fill me with hope and love; let this tea bring the passion back to my love and me." Strain the liquid and sip it while you visualize the heat you two will bring to the bedroom.

These are just a few of the potions that can be made for different occasions. It would be impossible to list them all. Imagine asking for a list of every recipe in the world. You have your ingredients, you know the power they bring, and now you have the confidence to make your own magical potions, salves, and tinctures. Providing your ingredients are safe, your potions will be. Have fun and experiment with your workings; remember to note the recipes so you can add them to your grimoire or Book of Shadows when they work.

Chapter 5: Magical Swords and Daggers

Norse trolldom is a place where fighting and battles are all part of life. The gods and goddesses fought hard, loved with passion, and used weapons to increase their chances of winning. Today we recognize that the most powerful weapons in our arsenal are intelligence, knowledge, morality, and truth. However, this doesn't mean that the historical weapons of trolldom aren't relevant. They show the passion behind the stories, beliefs, and the force of nature that drives the magic. Plus, the stories are meant to be dramatic and filled with mighty battles, including some of the most fantastic weapons crafted by mystical creatures and endowed with magical powers.

Weapons from Mythology and Norse Practices
The Trident

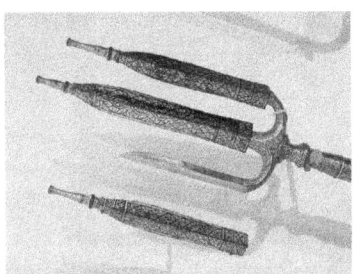

Tridents are usually weapons of sea gods.
https://commons.wikimedia.org/wiki/File:Trident,_Burmese,_18th_century.JPG

The three-pronged spear is named from the Latin words for three teeth. It is traditionally the weapon of the sea gods, especially Poseidon or Neptune. In the story of Poseidon, the Cyclops and the king of the sea forged the trident and then used it to strike a rock to provide water for the Acropolis in Athens. In Roman mythology, Neptune uses the weapon to strike the earth and produce the first mythical horse of war to pull the warrior's chariots in battle.

The trident appears in other mythology, including Indian and Jewish teachings. In Hindu mythology, the goddess Kali and the god Shiva are often pictured with a trident representing three important concepts of the religion.

Arondight

A famous character in Arthurian legend, Lancelot, was the lover of Queen Guinevere and a famous knight of the round table. His sword was named after the phrase "The unfading light of the lake."

Ascalon

St. George used the Ascalon sword to slay the dragon. Its name has been used in numerous video games in the creation of magical weapons in fantasy realms.

Caladgolg

The Ulster hero Fergus mac Roich wielded this mighty sword to create colorful arcs when he slew his opponents. His followers knew he had been successful when they saw the rainbow-like arcs formed by his sword.

Dainsleif

The Norse King Hogni used this weapon to inflict wounds that never heal. It was forged by the dwarves in return for gold and was considered to be one of the deadliest weapons in mythology.

Excalibur

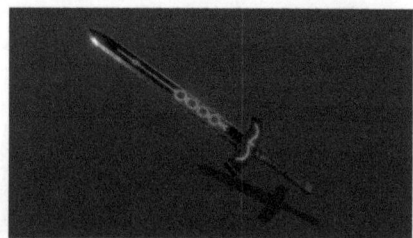

The Excalibur is thought to be imbued with magical powers.
Beto Alarcon, CC BY 4.0 <https://creativecommons.org/licenses/by/4.0>, via Wikimedia Commons: https://commons.wikimedia.org/wiki/File:3D_model_of_Excalibur_Morgan_(Fate_stay_night)_2019-11-12.png

The sword of King Arthur was pulled from the stone to determine who should rule England. Different stories have multiple legends regarding the stone, which was thought to be imbued with magical powers.

Fragarach

The magical sword of Nuada is a famous figure in Irish mythology. It was forged by the ancient Celtic gods and could inflict wounds that would never heal and also command the weather. It could also force the opponent to speak the truth when the blade was held against its opponent's throat.

Gambanteinn

A legendary wand-like dagger that appears twice in the Poetic Edda in Norse mythology. It was given as a gift to Harbaror when he outwitted a giant in one poem. In another poem, the dagger was used by Skirnir to threaten the giantess Gerd with her father's death if she refused to stop her wandering and stay away from the human realm.

Gram

The sword of Sigurd was used by the legendary Germanic hero of Norse mythology. He drew the sword from a tree trunk at a feast where a stranger had placed it. Unknown to the revelers, the stranger was Odin in disguise, and the sword was Gram. Everybody tried but failed until it came to Sigmund, who drew the sword with ease. Everybody coveted the sword, and Sigmund fought many battles to keep it safe. During one battle, Odin split the sword into two pieces, and Sigmund's wife took the parts and hid them.

When Sigmund died, a dwarf named Regin came to teach his son Sigurd the ancient arts and how to battle the dragon Fafnir and claim the treasure it guarded. He helped Sigurd forge the two halves of the Gram sword together to use as a weapon against the dragon. He eventually killed Fenrir with a single blow to the left side. Because the victory was so impressive, the sword was burned alongside the body of Sigurd, and it was never mentioned in mythology after the funeral pyre was lit.

Hovod

The mythical sword of the guardian of the Bifrost. It was made from Heimdallr and was reputed to choose by whom it was owned. It represents the blessings and strengths of the gods and would also incorporate the personality of the user. It is referred to as the key to the Bifrost Bridge that joins the nine realms and the human world.

Laevatein

Some Norse believers consider this to be an actual sword, while others think it is the mistletoe projectile used to kill the golden god Baldr after Loki, the trickster god, tricked his mother into revealing his weakness.

Legbiter

The legendary sword of Magnus III of Norway. When the Men of Ulster killed him, his sword was sent home to his wife to signal his death.

Mistilteinn

The legendary sword of Hromundr Grippson in Icelandic mythology. He defeated the draugr, the Norse version of the walking dead, who owned the sword and went on to kill over four hundred men with it. The sword was once lost in the water following a magical spell but was later retrieved from a pike's stomach.

Naegling

A legendary sharp and gleaming sword from the poem of Beowulf from the Viking era. It is an unusual tale of a hero and his fight with an evil dragon where the sword broke, not because of the strength of the opponent but because of the strength of the hero.

Ridill

Another dwarf-crafted sword in Norse mythology is famous as the weapon that cut out the heart of the defeated dragon Fafnir to roast for the victorious Sigurd and his men.

Skofnung

A formidable sword with magical powers that was the weapon of the Danish king Holf Kraki. It was said to contain the spirits of the twelve best warriors of the age who had been killed in battle in its mighty shaft. The sword could inflict wounds that could not be healed, but it could also heal wounds that had been sustained in battle. It should never be drawn in direct sunlight and never in the presence of a woman. Is this a misogynist sword, or does it reflect the feeling that women should not be present on the battlefield?

The sword survived its original owner by over five hundred years and featured in tales until it was buried with its owner in 1073. The sword was a well-traveled weapon and even made a pilgrimage to Rome.

Tyrfing

Another magical Norse sword was first mentioned in the Poetic Edda and featured in a tale when Odin's grandsons captured two dwarves and forced them to make him a magical sword. It had a golden hilt, would never rust and could pierce stone and metal just as easily as cloth. The dwarves forged the sword but cursed it by declaring it would kill a man every time it was drawn and would eventually kill the owners.

Of course, these swords are mainly mythological, and some historical weapons feature magic and trolldom. If you get the chance to see these magnificent weapons, you should take it; a peek back in history will help you become inspired in your work.

Historical Swords

British Ceremonial Swords

Five swords are kept in the Tower of London, including the Sword of Stae, the Curtana, the Sword of Justice, the Sword of Temporality, and the Sword of Mercy. They are magnificent coronation swords with inset jewels and are made of solid gold. Their crimson straps are made of velvet with embroidery in gold.

Joyeuse

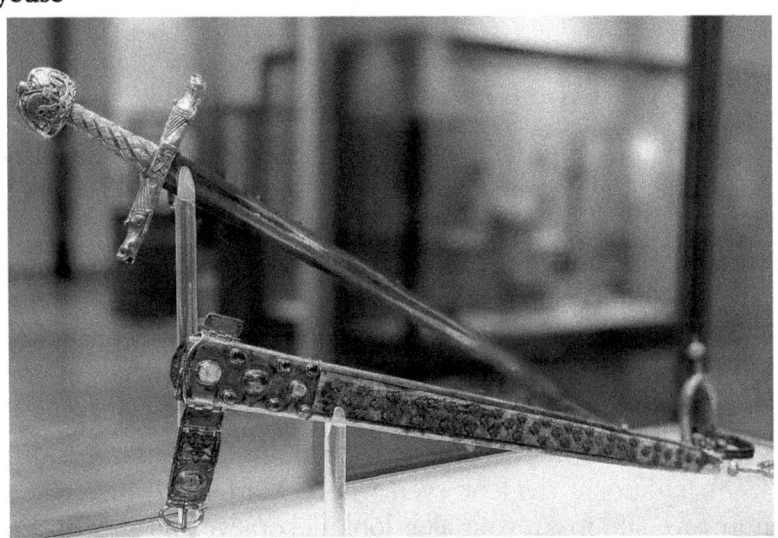

Joyeuse is Charlemagne's sword.
Louvre Museum, CC0, via Wikimedia Commons:
https://commons.wikimedia.org/wiki/File:%C3%89p%C3%A9e_du_sacre_des_rois_de_France,_dit_e_Joyeuse_-_Mus%C3%A9e_du_Louvre_Objets_d%27art_MS_84.jpg

The sword of the leader Charlemagne who was the first Holy Roman Emperor. It was moved to the Louvre following the French Revolution and has been used in French Coronation ceremonies ever since.

Lobera

The name means "wolf slayer," and it was the sword of the King of Castile in 1217. It was a sword of virtue and was bequeathed to his grandson on his deathbed.

The Sword of Essen

Given to the area of Essen to commemorate the sainthood of their warriors Cosmos and Damian. It can be seen at Essen Abbey in Germany.

This list of swords and daggers is far from inclusive, as weapons were a major part of mythology. The battle they fought and the victories and losses defined them and made them the legends of their mythology. Today magic has changed, and you need to use your strengths and powers instead of actual weapons.

Decorative daggers and knives can be used to decorate your altar and serve as channels for your energy and force. The athame is a Wiccan tool that can be used in your rituals and spells and can be bought from witchcraft outlets, or you can make your own. It should never be used for actual cutting as it is more powerful when used as a casting tool to direct energy.

History of the Athame

The first mention of the athame was in 1954 in a book published by Gerald Gardner, where he classed it as the witch's knife. He didn't describe the materials used or the exact use or size but just classed it as a magic weapon. In the 1980s, a more detailed description appeared in a book called the Spiral Dance. This book contained details of the perfect athame, described as a double-sided blade with a black handle. They suggested that the blade should be kept blunt for safety reasons, and the blade should be short and manageable.

In today's practice, the athame is used more like a wand and can be made from traditional steel or even wood. Marble athames and wands look impressive and make your altar look decorative and special. You can use many alternative objects as your athames, like a letter opener and a clay modeling tool. Decorate the handle and make your magic tool more personal.

Magical Staff

If you like the idea of a magical channel for your energy, you can replace your athame or wand with a staff. It is associated with authority and can make your magic more powerful. Like the wand, it is a powerful male symbol of energy and represents air and fire in elemental magic. Homemade staffs are far more effective than shop-bought staffs and are relatively simple to make.

Choose Your Wood

First, never cut a live piece of wood from a tree just because you like the look of the branch. Take a walk around a forest and look on the floor for a piece that has already fallen. The length should be between your shoulder height and the ground so you can wield it comfortably. The diameter should be around two inches so you can hold it firmly without breaking it.

You may like to choose the wood depending on its magical properties. Celtic magic has a dedicated Tree Calendar that the Druids created to explain the magical properties of trees.

The Tree Calendar

Dec 24th to Jan 20th, the Birch Moon

Birch represents rebirth; the birch is the first tree to regrow if a forest burns down. Birch protects and keeps the user safe and works with birch wands and staff to provide extra energy to spells.

Jan 21st to Feb 17th Is the Rowan Moon

Associated with Brigid, the goddess of the hearth and home, Rowan wood is also associated with self-improvement and travel. It is a powerful wood to encourage lost spirits' souls to move on and leave the astral plane.

Feb 18th to March 17th Is the Ash Moon

Yggdrasil, the mystical tree of life in Norse tales, was an ash tree. The wood can be used to encourage inner journeys and astral traveling. It protects you from the spirits that may harm you and all forms of negative energy. Use the ash wood to induce prophetic dreams to tell you what lies ahead for you in both professional and personal matters.

March 18th to April 14th Is the Alder Moon

Alder wood is often found by riverbeds and is believed to form the bridge between the heavens and earth. It connects the user to the faerie world and encourages them to help your work become more successful. Alder wood is used to make whistles to summon the air spirits and can be made into magical musical instruments.

April 15th to May 12th Is the Willow Moon

The willow is a tree of mystery and protection. It is often found near cemeteries to protect the dead, and the wood can bring protection to your spells. Use willow wood to encourage healing and growth.

May 13th to June 9th Is the Hawthorn Moon

Hawthorn wood is steeped in male potency, and its wood can be used to promote fertility and conception. The wood has a potent phallic feel and can be a powerful way to attract passion and love.

June 10th to July 7th Is the Oak Moon

The mighty oak towers over the other trees in the forest and is a sacred tree to Druid magic. Use the wood to fashion a staff to give protection and promote success and financial luck. It helps to cast a spell for success in business and work situations.

July 8th to August 4th Is the Holly Moon

The evergreen Holly tree symbolizes immortality and the circle of nature. Use it to bring good luck and safety to your magic and bring a sense of communing with nature to your work.

Aug 5th to Sept 1st Is the Hazel Moon

Hazel switches are especially effective for dowsing and divination purposes. The wood is related to wisdom and knowledge and can be used to re-inspire artistic and creative projects. Use hazel to get your muse back and become involved with your dreams.

Sept 2nd to Sept 29th Is the Vine Moon

As we know, wine was a popular drink of the Norse gods and commoners. The wine is brewed from grapes that come from vines, so it is no surprise that the vine symbolizes both happiness and anger. When wine is imbibed, some people become euphoric while others grow wrathful and show their rage. Use the wood to span these emotions and add balance to your work. You must include dark and light aspects to get the most powerful magic in your life.

Sept 30th to Oct 27th Is the Ivy Moon

Ivy is a hardy plant that can exist even when the host plant has died, and the wood from ivy is the perfect way to celebrate the cycle of life and death. Use it to improve your love spells and remove toxicity from your life.

Oct 28th to Nov 23rd Is the Reed Moon

Not strictly a tree, but reeds are used to attract the souls of the dead. They are made into haunting instruments that can help you collaborate with spirits and conduct successful séances. Use a reed staff to celebrate your ancestors and ask for their wisdom in your work.

Nov 24th to Dec 23rd Is the Elder Moon

Elder wood is used to protect against demons and other negative energies. It helps you to rejuvenate yourself and your spirit.

While traditional daggers and swords are only used for decorations, you can still wield some powerful weapons in your magic. Use the knowledge of wood to forge impressive wands and staff to add potency and direction to your work.

Chapter 6: The Usage of Cord Magic

Witchcraft involves tools and magical objects that can be decorative or sacred but can also involve everyday objects. What do you think of when you say the word cord? Surely the most important cord of all is the umbilical cord. This is the magical piece of skin that keeps every baby healthy. It feeds the fetus, supplies it with oxygenated blood, and is still attached after birth. Cutting the umbilical cord is an important part of the birth process. The remnants of the baby's belly button cord stay with them throughout their lives as an important reminder of their ultimate connection with the woman who gave birth to them.

Cord magic is a powerful source.
https://unsplash.com/photos/0ujNS9PMFhM

When you use electrical instruments, the chord is the power source, and when we put on shoes, a cord is often used to make them secure. Cords are an intrinsic part of some of our most important instruments, and we have vocal cords to make our voices resonate. Cords are flexible and can be manipulated to suit our needs, making them an especially useful tool in magic. Cords bind and keep separate elements together, making them important in spell work.

The History of Cord Magic

Once again, we look to Gerald Gardner and his revival of the Wiccan practice in the 1950s in England. He refers to the Cingulim or the witch's cord which represents the basic measurements of the witch's body or a standard length of nine inches. Nine is an important number in magic, but the cords relating to individual magic are especially potent. Cords are issued to witches who are classed as teachers, and they remain the property of the coven until the witch dies or leaves the coven for personal reasons.

In religion, cords are part of rituals that concentrate on meditation or prayers. Catholicism involves a cord of beads known as the rosary that helps the person praying to count their blessings and concentrate on their devotions. In Buddhism, the Lama will bless cords for the wearer to bring luck and bless them with Buddha's spirit. They would be worn around the wrist until they wore out and fell off. The cords' colors would signify the blessing's meaning and make them more effective.

Cords can be used individually or together to form magical effects. They can be combined with knot magic to do spells for all areas of magic and to complete goals in all areas of your life. In the following sections, we will explore some of the more powerful ways to use knots and cords in magic. First, we will find out how to use color to add intention to your work and what the assorted colors mean in cord magic.

Colors of the Cords

If your spells are all-purpose, then use neutral tones and avoid color. White cords are easily available and can represent the beginning of a new era and the purity of new beginnings. Gray and white cords will help you practice your new skills without worrying about your magic being misinterpreted, but when you are ready to add color, use this chart to give focus and intention to your spell.

Black: Wisdom, casting out, banishing, protection, self-examination, dream work, and astral communication.

Blue: The color of the element water, cleansing, happiness, devotion, forgiveness, and calm.

Brown: The earth element, making dreams happen, building relationships, forming roots, making financial decisions, and connecting with nature.

Gold: Monetary success, masculinity, justice, good health, the power of persuasion, solar magic, God connections, sacred energy, and the power of plenty.

Green: Money and financial success, natural magic, working with herbs, creativity, growth, and physical success.

Indigo: The spiritual world, the Crown chakra, psychic development, prophecy, self-realization, and connecting with the Divine self.

Lavender: Calmness, peace of mind, higher understanding, and learning.

Orange: Harvesting ideas and knowledge, motivation, energy, self-exploration, mental strength, hope, forward-thinking, creativity, and the power to adapt.

Pink: Self-love, new relationships, romance, forgiveness, friendship, and developing a more caring attitude.

Purple: Global issues, inclusivity, leadership, mystery, wisdom, luck, and liberation.

Red: The fire element, cleansing, new beginnings, sexual success, fertility, vitality, positive energy, and passion.

Silver: The feminine energy of the moon, connecting with the earth and her feminine energy, interpreting dreams and astral traveling.

Yellow: The air element, happiness, solar energy, increased focus, trust, self-confidence, new goals, improved memory, and inspiration.

Numerology in Cord Magic

If you incorporate cord magic with knot magic, you'll use numerology to make your spells more focused. The number of knots you use helps you add symbolism and intent to your work and make your results more impressive. Various numerology interpretations depend on cultural influences, but this simple reference list will help you get started. As you become more experienced, you can change the representation of the numbers to suit your subjective experiences. For instance, your birth date or lucky number may become an important part of your equation.

One: The higher being, the masculine energy, and the ultimate symbol of your willpower and your ability to influence your world.

Two: The sacred partnership and feminine energy, the power of duality and reconciliation, kindness, and sensuality.

Three: Youth, casting off adult worries, the power of play, action, happiness, humor, forward-thinking, and dreams.

Four: Laying foundations, responsibility, being part of a team, ethics, morality, financial stability, and caution.

Five: Opportunities, new projects, adventure, the strength of courage, frivolity, global inclusion, and awareness.

Six: Healing, mending relationships, true love, binding, support, and the power of teamwork.

Seven: Spirituality, heightened perception, knowledge, wisdom, the strength to survive, clear thinking, forward-looking, and optimism.

Eight: Responsibility, judgment, seeking power, authority, and leading from the front.

Nine: Humanity, benevolence, charity, responsibility, and awareness.

These nine numbers combine to form multiple numbers in magic and can be described by a simple incantation that witches and magic practitioners have adopted for hundreds of years.

Knot Incantation

"By the knot of just one, the magic has been spun,
  By the knot known by two, the meaning is true,
  By the knot we call four, the spell is deemed pure
  By the knot of the five, the spell comes alive,
  By the knot called six, the magic is fixed,
  By the knot numbered seven, the word is sent to the heavens,
  By the knot I call eight, I have sealed my spells fate,
  By the knot we call nine, all magic shall be mine."

Materials You Can Use for Cord Magic

Your basic materials set the intention for your spells. Here are some suggestions for the use of more diverse materials to make your spell personal:

- **Chains:** thin metal chains from jewelry can center your intentions if your spell is for someone else or yourself by using treasured chains from your jewelry box or heirlooms.
- **Floss:** Dental floss is a colorful and inexpensive way to use alternative cordage.
- **Laces:** Shoelaces, laces from corsets, or other clothing will make the spell concentrate on the owner.
- **Leather:** Supple strips of colored leather make your work more durable and long-lasting.
- **Ribbon:** The choice is immense, with ribbons of all widths, lengths, and colors available from local sources.
- **Thread:** Cotton threads are easy to use but can be delicate.
- **Twine:** Colorful and durable.
- **Wire:** Craft wire is a straightforward way to use metal forms of cord to provide a hardwearing way to create knots.

If you do choose fabrics, stay away from synthetic materials. They will be less effective than natural materials, absorbing the magical intentions more thoroughly and retaining their energy. Use wool, silk, or other natural ingredients rather than nylon or other synthetic materials.

The Intentions behind Cord Magic

Cord magic is a strong way to bind energies together, and when you use certain colors and numerology combined to direct the magical energies. It can be used for all applications and uses and is one of the most versatile types of magic available.

Protection Spell

Use the cords to bring negative energy to your work and keep it wrapped in your finished cord work. Use red, white, silver, or black cords and the numbers six and eight. Anoint your cords with the essential oil you feel protected by, sage and pine perhaps, and use pine needles to provide a base to work on.

Take the cords and weave them together to form a rope while you recite the following:

"These cords are my purity, and they will keep me safe from darkness. Make them strong and pure to keep me from the energy they keep secure."

Now imagine all the negativity in your life becoming trapped by the cords and disappearing from your life. Now imagine a blinding white light bathing your work area in purity. Once the rope has been formed, secure the ends tightly and place it where you feel safe. Take it with you when you leave the house or leave it in place to guard your space.

Binding Spell

If you are troubled by a certain person or situation, you can create a powerful cord to break the connections that bring you strife.

Take a cord that feels personal to you and represents your energy or use a combination of colors and materials; the choice is yours.

Make a knot in the cord and say, *"I cast you from my life* (insert name or situation) *my joy you will no longer steal."*

This is your binding knot and should stay knotted no matter what.

The second knot should happen underneath the first and is done as you say, *"I banish you (insert name) from my earthly life, freeing myself from all of your strife."*

The third knot should then be tied, saying, *"I cast you out (name) on this knot number three; your power will nevermore affect me."*

The fourth knot should be tied, saying, *"I expel you (name) from my memory and dreams and pray this charm will keep me safe."*

Keep the cord in a safe space and anoint it with your oils or crystals. If you feel any negativity returning, undo the first three knots and repeat the process. Never undo the binding knot, as you will release the negativity which may have increased.

Cooperation

If you struggle with other people being difficult and crave more balance and harmony in your life, trust simple cord magic. Choose several cords to represent the people causing you difficulties and name them. Make the cords form a braid as you concentrate on the people and situations they represent.

Say this incantation as you work: *"I call on the universe to create harmony between these elements, help us bring together our individual strengths and skills to form a team. I thank the powers that be for their cooperation and love."*

Creating Strong Ties

When you want something to happen, you should use cord magic to encourage it to happen. For instance, if you are applying for a job, create a cord union between yourself and the position you want.

Take a cord to represent yourself and one for the job. Weave them together as you say the phrase, *"I want this job, and I deserve it, let magic help me show my true self and how I fit the position."* Remember, if you get the job and then leave, don't forget to undo the knot.

Love and Marriage

Pagans and Wiccan ceremonies often include handfasting and ribbons to bind couples. Trolldom embraces all pagan rites and encourages using brightly colored ribbons and cords to signify the union. For friendship purposes, make simple colored bracelets to give to your friend to signify your connection. Using colors and patterns to show love is a decorative way to signify affection.

Good Luck Cords

The options are innumerable for making a lucky charm cord. Use your knowledge of the significance of colors and numbers to create a lucky cord. Use green cords for money and pink for love, and add beads or stones to create a decorative item for your altar. The sky is the limit; you can create as many as you like.

Use cords to add magic to physical objects. For example, when job hunting, take the business card of any companies you want to work with and add your resume to the bundle. Wrap the cord of your choice around the papers and say the following, *"Luck and prosperity be mine, make these people see me shine."* Now store the cord and bundle in a safe place and contact the companies. Then just wait for the interviews to start rolling in.

Self-Improvement

Create decorative cords to represent the areas of your life that need improvement. If your love life is hectic, use red or pink. If your finances are suffering, use green. Tie the separate cords around your wrist and use them to focus when you are dealing with your issues. Just touching the relevant cord will bring your focus to the forefront and energize you.

Weather Magic

Witchery based on weather has been used for generations. In Norse times the weather influenced every part of life, and it was important to influence it in any way possible. Sailors would create a strong cord with three knots to indicate the strength of the required winds. One knot represents a breeze, two represent a sailing wind, and three for a gale. Farmers would use a similar method to represent rain; one knot is a shower, two a steady rain, and three a full-on downpour.

However you use them, knots and cords are a simple and available way to practice magic. Beginners can experiment with their materials and create colorful and decorative magical pieces to wear or display in their sacred spaces. Having fun is an intrinsic part of the magic process, and cord magic is lots of fun.

Chapter 7: Unlocking Elf Magic

Elves play an important role in Norse mythology and are a race of beings who seem to encapsulate the beautiful features of humans but who can quickly turn and become wrathful. They seem to be perfect and live a magical life dancing in the woods and frolicking with the creatures that live there, but on closer examination, they merely reflect what we expect from perfect beings. Once you step into their realm, you incur their wrath and will soon fall ill or begin to develop symptoms of a disease. No matter how you apologize and try to retreat, it doesn't work. You have been elf-shot, and the repercussions are severe and sometimes deadly.

Elves play an important role in Norse mythology.
https://pixabay.com/es/illustrations/cl%c3%a1sico-arthur-rackham-victoriano-1722318/

Elves in Mythology

Tales from Denmark, Scandinavia, and other Nordic areas are filled with elven references. They are described as fair creatures who are luminous in their appearance and seem to remain youthful for hundreds of years. If they do age, it is at a slow rate unperceivable to human eyes, and they are often referred to as "the white people." They are mercurial characters who appear to be friendly to their human cohorts but are quick to anger if they believe they are under threat. Their punishments include illness, night terrors, physical attacks, and cruel pranks played on their victims. However, when humans feel ill with natural diseases, they often turn to elves to help cure them.

European mythology contained stories of elven birth and the need for human midwives and wet nurses. It is believed that when an elf gives birth, the only way the child will survive is with human help. The elves would choose a skilled midwife who would often be married to a preacher to return to the elven world with them, accompanied by a series of wet nurses who had recently given birth to their own children.

This group of women would stay in the elven realm until the child was deemed healthy enough to survive without their help. This raised concerns for women who could potentially be called upon to fulfill the role because if they ate or drank any food in the elven world, they would be prevented from returning to Earth. Any hospitality given and received meant they would be banished to spend the rest of their lives among the elves. It is unclear if the women were given any choice about their journey, but there are numerous tales of women keeping packed food and water just in case they were called to attend an elf birth.

The Story of Peter Rahm

A preacher named Peter Rahm was married to a midwife, which was a common pairing at the time. Mystical elves summoned her to attend their child's birth and help them deliver the baby. She agreed and traveled to the elven realm, where she performed her duties. When she was there, the grateful parents offered her food and drink, which she gracefully refused. They offered her a bed to rest in and water to wash with, both of which she refused. Once her duties were completed, she returned to the Rahm household. The following day the couple found a bag containing pieces of silver, a gift from the elves for her ministrations.

A Cautionary Tale of the Midwife and the Elf

A Danish tale tells of an elf visiting Earth on Christmas Eve to seek the help of a midwife to attend the birth of his child. The birth was successful, and the midwife stayed with the elf wife while the husband took the newborn child away to trick a newlywed human couple into giving away their fortune for his child. While her husband was away, the wife told the midwife to refuse any hospitality she was offered while she was in the elven realm. She explained that she had been a mortal woman who had worked as a midwife but made the error of accepting food while attending the birth. Because of this, she could not return to her human realm and was cursed to spend the rest of her life with the elves. The midwife followed her instructions and could return to Earth once the husband returned.

Elves and Relationships with Humans

As with most Norse tales, relationships often span diverse groups of beings and lead to offspring. Odin, Loki, and other deities often dabbled with other beings to produce some of the most memorable children in mythology. Sex, love, and passion are the driving forces in most of the Norse tales, so mating with creatures who are so beautiful is inevitable. Some tales tell of elves seducing unwitting humans into having sex with them, while others tell of love stories and consensual pairings. The children from these unions are often incredibly attractive and go on to do remarkable things.

These half-human and half-elven children appear to live human lives and are often destined to be great healers and well-versed in magical powers. They appear to be benevolent creatures who are both beautiful inside and out. In ballads and tales of these unions, the human partner will often have to fulfill a task to win the hand of their elf bride. One popular task was to visit the elf realm and rescue a human who had been trapped there to win their spouse's hand in marriage.

Wayland the Smith

Perhaps the most famous elf in Norse mythology is Wayland the smith, known as Volund in the ancient texts. He appeared in a Scandinavian tale around the ninth century BC when he was featured in a story about king Nithuth and his terrible fate.

The elf and his brother take wives who are part of the Valkyries who stay with them for a couple of years but then fly away. The brother sets off on a mission to find them while Wayland stays home and forges a series of rings enhanced with gems to present to his wife when she returns. King Nithuth hears of his labor and visits the elf's home as he sleeps. The king took the most beautiful ring and left. When the elf awoke, he thought his wife had returned, only to discover the ring had been stolen. He visits the king's palace and reclaims his treasure.

The king then accuses the elf of theft and gives his sword and treasures to his wife and daughter. He cuts the elf's hamstrings and banishes him to a deserted island with instructions to craft precious objects for the king for the rest of his life. Nithuth's sons visit the island to see the objects the elf has created and are killed by the vengeful elf, who then makes cups from their skulls and gems from their eyes while he fashions a brooch from their teeth. The king's daughter visits Wayland to ask him to mend her ring, the one he originally made for his wife. The pair drink together, and the princess falls asleep in the chair. Wayland then makes her his lover, and she is bound to him when she falls pregnant.

There is a gap in the story, but it seems that king Nithuth then summons the crafty elf to explain what happened to his sons and his daughter. Wayland makes the king swear no harm will come to him or his pregnant wife, the princess, before he confesses to killing the two princes. The king agrees, and the story concludes with the elf and his bride flying away and staying safe.

The Tale of Tam Lin

Although it originated in Scotland, the tale of Tam Lin travels well through Europe. It is based on the elf Tam Lin being captured by the queen of the fairies and eventually being rescued by a mortal girl. Tam is a crafty elf who claims the virginity of any maiden who passes through his forest, which includes a young maid called Janet. She returns home, finds out she is pregnant – and challenges the elf about her condition.

She is determined to keep the baby but is forced to take a herb that will induce her to miscarry. She returns to the forest where Tam Lin lives to find the herb and questions the elf about his origins. He tells her he was once a mortal man who fell from his horse, was captured by the fairy queen, and held against his will. He tells her he is scheduled to become a sacrifice to the gods of hell on Halloween, and they devise a plan to rescue him.

Tam tells Janet he will be riding a white horse, and she must pull him off the horse and catch him to rescue him from his deadly fate. He warns her the fairies will turn him into all manner of beasts to force her to drop him, but he won't harm her. The night of Halloween arrives, and Janet waits in the forest for the elven parade. She spots Tam on his white horse and pulls him from the saddle. When she catches him, the fairies turn him into a series of beasts, but she still keeps hold of him. They turn Tam into a red-hot piece of coal, and she is forced to cast him into the well.

She hides him from the fairies when he emerges as a naked human man. The queen is angry but agrees that Janet has fulfilled her task and lets Tam return to his mortal form. The pair leave the forest together and live happily ever after.

Isabel and the Elf Knight

Of course, this is mythology; not all tales are filled with love and happiness. The elfin knight was a handsome elf with beatific features and a seemingly kind demeanor. He blew into his horn and declared his love for Lady Isabel, whose heart is won over. She agrees to travel with him to the greenwood to marry him and have his children.

It all changed when the pair arrived at the wood, and the elf knight showed his true colors. He told Isabel he had already killed seven princesses to amass his fortune, and he was planning to kill her to steal her treasures and make her his eighth victim. However, Lady Isabel is a smart cookie and tells the elf she realizes she has been beaten. She tells the elf to rest his head on her knee and spend some time together before she meets her fate. He does so, and she lulls him to sleep with a song, binds him with his own belt, and then kills him with a knife.

Elf Folklore

There have been many representations of elves and their powers in the past, but they differ in certain cultures and mythology. They are mystical creatures who can cause illness and cure them. They are linked to changelings by stories of elves who favored human babies over their own, especially ones born to parents with fair features. The tale suggests that the tithe to hell that had to be paid every seven years meant they could sacrifice a changeling rather than one of their own.

When the elves stole a human baby, it was believed they left an elf baby behind, which was then identified as a changeling. The infant may appear to be human, but they had strange afflictions that identified them as changelings. The most recognizable symptom was their need to eat more than human babies, which signaled a serious dilemma for the parents. They often chose to kill the baby before it could develop into a child to ensure the changeling caused them no harm.

This may seem chilling to us today. Babies were killed for being different, but back then, there were no other explanations for children being unusual. People believed that supernatural forces ruled their lives and blamed them for any abnormalities.

Norwegian folklore tells of the spirits of the dead returning in elf form. The tale of Olaf the Holy sees his ancestors returning to the grave of Norway's first saint to find an elf residing there. They believe it is the spirit of the old king and erect a signpost at the burial ground reading "Olaf the elf of Geirstad."

Elves' true magic seemed to explain strange events like the birth of a baby with deformities or illnesses that seemingly had no origin. They were blamed for the most unusual events, and the prefix elf was attached to even mundane problems to explain why they happened. For instance, if a person's hair became knotted or tangled around a random object, it was called an elf-knot.

Today we have more scientific and modern explanations for unusual events and do not need to explain them away with supernatural reasoning, but that shouldn't stop us from being interested in elves. In Iceland, they believe so strongly in elves and their underground realm that in 2012 a law was passed to stop construction on a road that would pass through an area believed to be the habitat of elves. The protest was taken to the highest courtroom and led to an enforced law forbidding any interference in areas believed to be inhabited or of significance to elves anywhere in Iceland.

We still believe in elves at Christmas and picture the little green men and ladies helping Santa at the North Pole make presents for the world's children. Who can forget the portrayal of Will Ferrel playing Buddy the elf in the classic movie Elf? It is far removed from the Nordic version of the beautiful creatures described in their mythology but still relevant. Elves' magic seems to be their trickery, playfulness, and belief in themselves. Surely, the best way to adopt your elf magic is to be industrious, seek the best for yourself, and keep faith in whatever you believe in.

Chapter 8: Dwarf Magic

Dwarves are practical creatures, and although they live in a world of magic and witchcraft, they only believe in practical magic. They dismiss all other forms of magic as sorcery and forbid themselves and other dwarves from practicing it. Although they have links with the elves, there is a bitter dispute over their use of healing magic and potions. Dwarves only trust magic they have control over and magic that produces things. They despise the sea and heavens and would never live anywhere other than areas with healthy resources they can utilize in their work.

Dwarves don't use the term magic but attach the practice to their preferred term of crafting. In this way, dwarves practice craft magic and produce the most amazing objects in mythology. Theirs is a magic of things, and they have their own way of making seemingly everyday materials into magical and wondrous objects. Some Norse believers see elves as magical beings, gnomes are master craftsmen, but dwarves exceed them in their knowledge and skills. They are short, squat creatures with misshapen and ugly features, but their minds are filled with mysteries and wonder. They knew Newton's laws way before Newton and intrinsically understood the laws of dynamics and thermodynamics. They used this knowledge to make themselves indispensable to the gods and goddesses who would repeatedly call on them to produce their jewelry, weapons, and other magical objects.

Worthy Dwarves from Norse and Scandinavian Mythology

There are so many references in Norse mythology that it would take another book to list them all and their importance. The Prose Edda and the Poetic Edda are littered with tales of the dwarves and how they played a significant role in Norse beliefs, but here we can study just a few of them and get an idea of the part they played in society.

Alberich appears in Germanic tales from the medieval poems known as the Thidriksaga, where he is described as the king of supernatural beings.

Austri is one of the four dwarves tasked with holding the skull of Ymir aloft to form the heavens.

Billingr was the father of a young girl who was the object of Odin's lust. He told the god to return that night and claim his prize, but when Odin returned, he found the path blocked by hounds and warriors. Undeterred, Odin returned the next morning to find a female dog tied to the maiden's bed. The lowly dwarf had outwitted the mighty Odin and saved his daughter from her fate.

Durim is the second dwarf ever created and the leader of the powerful group of dwarves known as the monsignor.

Fjalar was one of a pair of dwarves who slew Kvasir and converted his blood into the liquid that formed mead which has inspired scholars and poets ever since.

Galar was the other dwarf who helped Fjalar kill Kvasir.

Ivaldi belongs to a group of skillful dwarves who fashioned vessels for the gods and goddesses. They are acclaimed for their work on the ship the Skipbladnir for Freya and the golden locks they made to replace the hair of Sif when Loki tricked her. They are also the experts behind the sword of Odin.

Mondul was the master behind some of the sturdiest axles, shafts, and handles on the gods' chariots.

Norori supports the northern point of the skull of Ymir that forms the heavens.

Sindri was a dwarf that was so respected Odin used his name as an alternative term for the place where dead souls would gather.

Skirfir is the dwarf of paneling who could create the most sturdy and decorative work from herringbones.

Suori holds the southern point of the skull of Ymir.

Uri was the keeper of the smithy and head of the blacksmiths. He was also known as King of the Slag.

Vestri holds the western point of the skull of Ymir.

This list is far from comprehensive, and the lands where they lived are also referenced throughout Norse teachings. The dwarves are enigmatic and secretive about their skills and prefer to work far from prying eyes. The bulk of their crafting involves simple objects with magical elements, and the forge where they are created is a sacred place.

The Craft

Although dwarves were mainly involved with mundane work when they were called to "craft" certain items, four individual elements were involved. A specialized forge was formed using algebraic calculations, the character of the crafter, the material used, and the construction methods. All these elements made each forge special and personal to the dwarf who used it. Another noteworthy element of dwarfish crafting is the Kunzler, or the primary dwarf craftsman. He would normally have a Knecht working with them, a Norse version of the apprentice, and the master dwarf was known as the Kunzler.

The tools they used were bequeathed to them by their master or were crafted by their own hands, and the dwarves were very wary of their knowledge being abused by outsiders. They formed their own guilds and only allowed trusted members of the community to join them, and they never wrote their knowledge in books or other texts. The apprenticeship was long and arduous, and only the most gifted dwarves would complete it and become Kunzler's themselves.

Dwarf Worlds

There is little natural light in the world of the dwarf. They don't see black as a shade, just a state of being. There is darkness in the world that lies under the stone and shade that lies beneath the light. The brightest part of the dwarf world is the flame from their sacred forge. Dwarf hell is a place where they cannot function. It is a world of mute paralysis where the air is dank and cold, and the souls that live there will never feel warmth again.

The dwarf ethos is based on gems, stones, and precious metals, and while humans and gods would refer to the beauty of a gem or precious stone, the dwarf would know the complete history of every piece they use in their craft. Every material has a history that goes deep and includes where it was originally mined, who found it, and how its past has shaped it. A reverence makes the finished items so magical they are highly sought after by all.

This brings us to the final element of the dwarf magic, payment. In all the Norse myths, dwarven magical items cost potential owners a high price which could be money, gold, or debt of favor the dwarf could use to boost their social position.

Modern Dwarf Magic

Today we see dwarves as fictional creatures that feature in fantasy stories and as underground creatures who do their work in secret and play their part in the tales that feature them. But what if we consider their ethos in more practical forms? Can we perform dwarf magic and become Master of Physical transformation?

Yes, we can. There are so many resources available to learn from that we can emulate the dwarf magic from Norse mythology. Create beautiful and sacred pieces to use in your own form of craft magic and bring the energy of these magical creatures. If dwarves existed today, they are the most likely form of Norse creature that would blend in. They are humanoid and industrious and would contribute to society.

Study Gemstones and Crystals to Use in Your Magic

Nature's magic is all around you, and knowing the properties of certain items will boost your spells and rituals. Build an impressive collection that will be useful and beautiful.

Agate

A brown or gold stone agate is used to boost magic related to mental issues like discovery, healing, and overcoming mental health issues. It will bring you energy and help you overcome any loneliness or sadness you may be experiencing. Carry it with you to bring energy to your day, or place it under your pillow to make your sleep more restful and freer from bad energy.

Amethyst

A colorful purple crystal amethyst is connected to the element of water and is used to sharpen the mind. Use it to cleanse your sacred areas and create a light and sacred space. Ancient Greek practitioners used the crystal to avoid inebriation, so carry it in your pocket if you are on a night out to avoid any possible drunkenness.

Bloodstone

A green stone with specks of red and gold, this powerful stone will bring solar energy and connect you to the planet Mars. It has deep connections to the blood and is used to soothe blood disorders or to calm menstrual issues. If you are trying to conceive, carry a bloodstone or use it in fertility rituals to improve your chances of falling pregnant.

Carnelian

Carnelians are used in grounding spells and rituals.
jaja_1985, CC BY 2.0 <https://creativecommons.org/licenses/by/2.0>, via Wikimedia Commons: https://commons.wikimedia.org/wiki/File:Carnelian_-_tumble_polished_stone.jpg

The red/orange hue of the carnelian streaked with white is comparable to the landscapes found in the American southwest area. It is associated with the element earth and is used in grounding spells and rituals. It is a potent fertility stone and can be sued to treat impotency and infertility. Use carnelian to keep your magic tools free from negative energy and create a talisman from carnelian to use as a magic shield.

Diamonds

Tied to both elements of air and fire, they are also linked with solar energy and the heavens. Although they are almost always flawed, they still have powerful energy and can be used to promote astral communications and fortune-telling. It also enhances meditation and is used in rituals to promote Intuition and mental clarity.

Garnets

These blood red and sometimes purple have strong connections to the element of fire and the eternal goddess. However, they are a strong female-related gem that can be used in all manner of spells. Use garnets to uncover the mysteries of the female body and deal with any female issues. Be aware that garnets that have been obtained through deception or theft carry a curse that remains until they are returned to their rightful owner. Garnets are especially important in balancing energies and connecting the physical and spiritual parts of the human psyche.

Iron Rose

Also known as the hematite, this is one of the most important stones you can have in your collection. It is used in Feng Shui to create safe spaces so you can use it to protect your home and sacred area. Place it on your windowsill and above your door to create a safe environment. Carry iron rose stones with you to encourage psychic communications and drive out stress. It will improve your confidence and make you more decisive and successful.

Jade

Used in Eastern magic, jade is a stunning green stone that can appear to be white, gray, or even pink in different lights is a calming stone connected to the element of the earth. Use it to heal internal organs and bring a balanced feeling between your physical and spiritual energies.

Jasper

This is a robust stone that is brownish-red in color and flecked with other earthy hues. It is associated with the element earth and is used in healing therapies and rituals. It is perfect for grounding yourself and your space after a spell or ritual and can be used to center your energy. Its earthy energy is also associated with sexual potency, and it can help you put the oomph back in your sex life if you place it underneath your mattress.

Lazurite

Also known as lapis lazuli, this uniquely beautiful stone comes in an array of hues ranging from pale blue to the deepest shade of blue, just like the night sky, depending on where it was mined. The color is significantly reminiscent of the element water and is used to treat depression and relieve anxiety. Use it in your magic to encourage psychic connections and to commune with the Divine. Lapis lazuli is a calming element that will aid your mediation and help you reach altered states of consciousness. In Egyptian traditions, the lazurite was often used in funereal rituals and to decorate the sarcophagus.

Moonstone

As the name suggests, this stone has strong lunar connections and is intrinsically linked to the female deities that use lunar energy. It is the female energy that helps with menstrual and reproduction issues, and it brings a calm and soothing aura when carried. Use it in ceremonies to celebrate the power of Sol and Mani, the Norse god and goddess of the sun and moon. Carry it with you to help you feel calm and balanced, especially in times of stress.

Obsidian

Black and shiny, this stone has a certain presence and is used to draw the toxins from the blood and body. Use it by placing it beneath your feet while you perform energy work to draw out any negativity and harmful energy. It is strongly connected to the element fire and should be used in rituals for intuition and scrying.

Opal

Often described as an unlucky stone, the opal has often been misunderstood. It comes in a range of shades ranging from luminescent and pale to dark blue with green and yellow specks. In certain lights, they look like they are lit from within and are especially stunning in candlelight. It links all four elements, making it an essential part of your magic stone collection. Use it to protect your physical space and heal your psychic energy. It has a powerful absorption quality, drawing in both positive and negative forces, making it a powerful enhancer when used in magic.

Quartz

There are so many kinds of quartz it is hard to choose which to focus on. Choose rose quartz for romance or white quartz for more general work. The stones are all connected to the four elements and are versatile and powerful when used in healing and protection. They promote spiritual and divine growth and will help you connect to the universe.

Sapphires

Their regular color is blue, but sapphires also come in white and yellow. They are associated with water and bring the energy that helps you connect to spirit guides and receive their messages.

Tiger's Eye

The coloring and black banding on this stone gives the impression you are looking into the eye of the tiger, which explains the name. It is connected to the element fire and used for general health spells and rituals. Incorporate it into your life to enhance your self-confidence and protect you from the negative forces of others.

Turquoise

Associated with Native American practices, this eye-catching stone is blue flecked with black or white. It is a powerful healing stone that brings knowledge and wisdom to whoever wears it.

Zircon

It looks like a diamond and can be used as a more affordable stone to create the same energy in magic. It has strong sexual energy and is used in rituals for improving relationships and fertility.

Chapter 9: A Guide to Practicing Trolldom

The practice in this book is designed to help you live better and become the person you want to be. Norse beliefs and trolldom allow you to make choices and be the architect of your own fate. They encourage you to trust your instincts, and this is why there is a significant shift in people choosing to eschew traditional religions in favor of the Nordic ways. They understand that choice and freedom of movement have been restricted for generations and that certain religions focus on fear and punishments as part of their doctrines and seek to rule them with fear and fixed rules.

Why should free-thinking people have to follow archaic rules that have no relevance in modern society? Nordic practices and pagan beliefs put the power back in your hands and give you the freedom to abandon monotheism and embrace a range of deities. Trolldom is a cover-all term for several practices we have covered and a whole lot more. You have no limits to stay within, and every day can be a learning experience. There are multiple resources for you to tap into, and you can get acquainted with like-minded people.

Traditional religions are constantly asking their followers to ask for forgiveness. Maybe their sexuality doesn't conform to the norm. The believers are asked to conform to boring, impoverished archaic rituals that aren't pleasant or fulfilling. Norse and Nordic rituals are filled with passion and beliefs fueled by your desires and needs. You can tailor the magic to work for you and make your life richer in all ways. Doesn't that sound much better than apologizing and asking for forgiveness about things that are beyond your control?

Nordic Societies

The Asatru Alliance

This is an American Heathen Group founded in 1994 that offers a safe place for pagans and heathens to meet, share ideas and gain knowledge. Kindreds across the world reach out to each other and practice the ancient Asatru, which predates Christianity and is the main religion that trolldom recognizes.

They offer courses on traditional skills and craftwork from the era and encourage their members to take part. They celebrate the power of mead and its significant role in rituals. They have an online calendar that tells followers what the special holidays are, the date they fall on, and highlights any kindred celebrating these dates.

There are links and resources for people to contact other communities that appeal to them. The Alliance is based in Arizona, but there are communities throughout the world that follow the Nordic ways. The movement began to gain interest in the 1970s and has grown exponentially ever since. It has become the biggest growing religion per capita in the last ten years and especially appeals to younger members of society.

Why Do the Figureheads in Nordic Beliefs Appeal to Followers?

They are fallible! Simply put, people can relate to them and their lives. Odin, the master of Asgard and the lord of the Norse people, made mistakes. He had affairs, and lower beings tricked him. His love life was complicated, and his children weren't always the best. Freya, Loki, Thor, and Bader are all part of our language thanks to popular culture, but even though the films bear little resemblance to the mythology, they have elevated interest in all things Norse. The whole Norse universe is filled with wonderous beings like the elves and dwarves we have already studied. The gods and goddesses were awe-inspiring and multifaceted. They could be benevolent, fearsome, cruel, or destructive depending on the situation, but they were never boring.

The tales from Norse mythology are filled with death-defying courage, and this is something we can all relate to. As we have already discovered,

Nordic religion has no hard and fast rules or doctrines, and trolldom is no different. It suggests that we can all improve and become more productive beings, but it lets us choose how to do that. The virtues that Nordic ways promote are no-brainers; it's just that modern society has caused us to forget the importance of doing the right thing. We are pushed to succeed at any cost, often at the expense of others. When did we get so ruthless that it is okay to trample on people just to become successful or wealthy?

Are fame, wealth, and material needs your driving force? Will you do anything to achieve your goals? Or do you strive to be successful while making the world a better place simultaneously? We can all be ambitious and reach for the stars but let's try to get back to some of the more noble virtues that held fast in the past. Before the advent of technology and industry, before the time when we expected to have everything we wanted with the least effort, there was a code to live by. A series of virtues that meant something to the Nordic people are experiencing a revival as we seek to embrace the values of simpler times.

The Nine Noble Values of the Viking Folk

Some people may question using Vikings to represent the nobility of the Norse age. Surely, they were bloodthirsty warriors who pillaged monasteries and committed unspeakable acts in foreign lands. That is one view, and, understandably, it is a common conception of the Viking hordes due to media portrayal, but when you study them more closely, there was much more to the Viking race than violence.

They lived in a civilized society that had structure and government. They held courts to decide what was right and how to deal with lawbreakers. Their children were taught noble arts, and both boys and girls were instructed in the art of fighting. They were pioneers who took to the seas to explore and seek new lands for their people, and, most of all, they were farmers. Their knowledge of the land was exemplary, and they had the skill to grow crops in even the bleakest environments. Remember, the Nordic lands are a hostile part of the world with cold and harsh climates and a lack of sunshine that makes even the hardiest crops difficult to cultivate, but the Vikings managed to make these lands fertile, and they thrived.

Vikings lived a warrior lifestyle, but they also embraced wisdom and virtues. They had a noble and true code that coincided with multiple other warrior codes throughout the world. This proves that there was a time when everyone recognized that true character and honor were universal. Following Nordic values may just help us get back to that time.

Courage

Bravery isn't just needed on the battlefield. It should be something we practice every day. Put your head above the parapet and be heard even when your opinion differs from the mainstream. Stand up for people who don't have a voice and be their champion. Bravery means challenging others and avoiding conforming because it seems like the easier option. Use your wisdom and discretion to choose your battles and avoid acting recklessly, making you look foolish. Be a warrior but fight for things you honestly believe in rather than battles that have already been lost.

Truth

Honesty seems to be a value that has fallen by the wayside. Lying and untruths are so commonplace they seem acceptable and part of getting what you want. In truth, lying is cowardly and means you can't face the truth. If you know something isn't true or don't believe it to be true, then say so. Don't go along with the lie because it is easier than being honest.

Everyone perceives things differently, and what is true for some may not be for others, and that's okay. The world would be dull if we all thought the same way, but you can be a warrior against lies and still have your own opinions. Live by your truth as far as you can, carry the banner against BS and respect others' rights to believe what they do. You set yourself on a path of lies when you lie to yourself. If you can't be true to yourself, then how can you be true to others?

There is a right way to do things, and, as a warrior, you must choose. The Viking code allowed their warriors to lie back if they were being lied to, challenging their opponents like for like gave them the upper hand. True honor isn't always straightforward; you must decide what is right according to your intentions and do the right thing. Honesty shouldn't be brutal, and discretion is the best part of valor.

Honor

How many people use the word honor anymore except in wedding vows? There are places of honor that mean they are important and worthy, or there is the quality of knowing what is right. Honors are given to those who do wonderful things, but when it comes to virtues, what we consider honorable matters. Honor is your internal moral compass and not your reputation.

Honor doesn't originate from what other people think of you it is all about what you think of yourself. Noble warriors who live by their moral code will have very few regrets. They have an honorable soul and will have lived ethically and morally sound lives.

Fidelity

Another seemingly archaic term, fidelity, simply means faithful. Most people associate this virtue solely with marriage, but when you apply it to the rest of your life, you fully understand why it is such an important virtue. Stay true to your friends, your family, and your partner. Viking families believed that if you attacked them, they were under an obligation to fight back. This is different from revenge and means fulfilling an obligation to show fidelity to others. Of course, in modern society, we don't believe in an eye for an eye mentality, and we rely on the law to put right wrongs against us, but that doesn't mean fidelity is a lost virtue.

Show fidelity by entering into a bond with those you hold dear. Let them know you will always be there for them and that you have their back. Never disrespect that bond, no matter what pressures you have to go against them. Be true to your gods, friends, and family; they will see you as a loyal and faithful ally. Take your time making these bonds and only give your fidelity to those who deserve it, as fidelity is a gift that shouldn't be given lightly.

Discipline

An old Nordic saying tells us, "He who lives without discipline dies without honor," which sums up what happens when we have no self-discipline. This is a tricky virtue as it sometimes means your code of ethics may differ from those that the government or other peers have dictated. Stand fast and be courageous with your choices, you won't perfect self-discipline overnight, and it takes a strength of conviction that will test you. Take control of your emotional responses and exercise self-discipline to gain control of your life.

Hospitality

Not the most obvious warrior trait, hospitality is nevertheless especially important to the Viking code. They believed that the gods and goddesses regularly visited earth and passed as mortals to evaluate them, and they didn't want to disrespect them should they meet. Viking households welcomed strangers and travelers into their homes and treated them with respect. This virtue is about your personal ethics, regardless of what others deserve. We should always behave to others like we would like them to behave to us.

Industriousness

Laziness wasn't allowed in Norse times. The land was a cruel mistress and needed to be worked to produce food. The seas were also dangerous to travel and would reward any lack of industry with cruelty and death. True warriors work hard and smart to use their time efficiently. This may seem obvious at work but does your industriousness only apply in the workplace? What about at home? Do you get in from work and expect everything to be done for you? Try becoming more productive in all areas of your life and reap the rewards.

Mediocre is a word that isn't included in Nordic work ethics. They believe that if you are going to do something, you should do it to the best of your abilities. Heighten your expectations, and others will follow. Lead by example and show the world what you are capable of, and your self-respect will grow, and so will your achievements.

Self-Reliance

Vikings didn't have the welfare state to call on; they believed that their family and friends needed them to survive. They believed that being responsible for your destiny and that of your close circle was down to individuals. When a group of warriors thinks like this, they are individually strong, and when they work as a group, they are invincible.

Too many people rely on others to survive. We seem to have lost that important feeling of self-reliance when you reap benefits stemming from your actions. There is a very selfish side to today's society where we seem to believe we are entitled to certain standards. Of course, how we live is different from the Nordic ways, but that doesn't mean we should expect other people to provide for our basic needs.

Try another way of thinking and be more self-reliant. Save your money for big purchases rather than relying on credit. Be frugal and enjoy the fruits of your labor by considering every cent you spend and appreciating the goods you earn. We all want the best for our families, but are we teaching them the right lessons when we rely on outside sources to provide? No, we aren't, and that needs to stop; bring up your kids to understand that good things come to those who rely on themselves and put in the effort.

Perseverance

Have you spotted a common theme in the previous eight virtues? They all need effort and will take time to master, so it seems inevitable that perseverance should apply to all of them and finish the list. There is no point in striving for self-improvement if you don't have the most important virtue: the power to get past obstacles or difficulties and continue, the doggedness to reach your goals or the strength to keep going when the going gets tough. **Perseverance.**

You aren't trying out a warrior's lifestyle for a laugh. Committing to the Nordic trolldom virtues is a lifelong pledge; you either have the qualities it takes, or you don't. No judgment is involved, not all humans are destined to be warriors, but if you have the steeliness of character to fail, get up from that failure, and carry on with the determination to succeed next time, then you are potential warrior material.

More Modern Ways to Live a Nordic Life

Did you know that in 2016 a report about the happiest places on earth, four of the top five countries were Nordic? Denmark topped the table, and Iceland, Sweden, and Finland came in at three, four, and five. Switzerland was second, and the US came thirteenth. The survey was based on happiness living in their societal structures, the freedom to make choices, the generosity of their compatriots, and their low levels of corruption. They also factored in the social support, GDP per head, and equality levels to calculate a happiness scale.

The US President at the time, Barack Obama, was so impressed with the results he suggested that the Nordic nations should be put in charge of running the world for a while so they could clean things up. So, it is no wonder that people are turning to trolldom, Asatru, and Nordic influences to make their lives better, and here are a few suggestions on how you can embrace the Hygge lifestyle, or what the people in the frozen north describe as the art of living well.

You may not be able to emulate the Nordic countries' equality in education, gender issues, and other societal facilities. Their egalitarian society ensures that every individual has access to the same facilities no matter their heritage. We can, however, Nordify our lives and make them more comfortable, healthy, and content.

Hygge

Hygge comes from the old Nordic word *hugr*, which means soul, mind, and consciousness. It isn't a fad and isn't all about embracing Scandinavian culture. It is about being in the present and appreciating what is happening around you. It doesn't happen on the Internet, but the global community can add to the experience. Sounds confusing? It isn't but let's explore how being at home with the ones you love is much more important than any other connections.

Another Scandinavian word to learn is *pyt*, which loosely translated means "forget about it" or "okay that happened, so let's move on" and is a breezy, happy way to develop a tricky situation into a positive one. Use it when someone apologizes for something trivial like spilling water on your carpet or catching your arm as you pass. PYT! Move on and get over it! Try it now and experience how good it feels not to sweat the small stuff.

Some people believe the Hygge lifestyle is all about white decorations, candles, huge cushions on a linen sofa, and natural materials decorating the home. It isn't about what you have or don't have; it's about how you live and your human interactions with others. Hygge is all about lack of ostentation and being content with what you have. This doesn't mean that you have no ambition but quite the opposite. Your ambitions are to have a balanced work-play relationship and know how to relax.

Where to Start

With yourself. Simple as that, take a good look at yourself and what you bring to the table. Are you able to let go of your ego and be yourself with other people? Can you laugh at yourself and be self-effacing? Hygge is about letting your hair down and being part of the moment. Stick your smartphone on hold and look people in the eyes as you toast them with a glass of wine, water, or whatever you have available and see what happens next.

Scandi Conversations

What are popular topics for Scandi hygge style talks? Anything spontaneous and not concerned with advancement. Don't concentrate on networking (possible the most anti-hygge word ever) or your future; just talk about what matters now. The last film you saw or a funny story about what happened when you went shopping last week. Imagine a Nordic village square filled with locals just chewing the fat about recipes, what is happening with the weather, or local fashions. They are conversations that would have been spontaneous and filled with laughter. Bonding over local issues can be so rewarding, and we have forgotten how to be spontaneous.

Serious conversations can happen, but they don't have to be a matter of life or death. Hygge provides a safe environment where people know they can air their opinions without fear of reprisals. All manner of subjects can be discussed and debated, and that is what Scandi conversations are all about, equality and respect. Why do some people believe happiness is linked to financial status when you look at those who have achieved it and are still unhappy? Scandinavian and trolldom are all about valuing human contact and interaction in their purest form and feeling energized by the company you keep.

Other Ways to Live Nordic Style

Get Viking Fit

We all want to get our bodies into shape, and Viking workouts are the perfect way to connect to the Nordic life and get outside more. Check out Scandinavian Fitness online and learn from a former Olympic rower, Linda, how to use crawling exercises, weights, and physical movements outside to get fit. She promises to get you sweaty and out of breath with some amazing results.

Eat Foods That Are in Season

We are all so used to having all foods no matter the season because we import all goods. Try another way of eating and choose foods and vegetables available to you from local sources. Try foraging and picking wild berries to make your food tastier and healthier. Nordic clean eating is a perfect way to hone your tastebuds to a new type of food cooked from scratch and filled with seasonal favorites.

Add more grains and fish to emulate a Scandi diet, and you will find the food more diverse, affordable, and available. It will help you lower your cholesterol and blood pressure with nutritious ingredients and vitamins. Try the Nordic Cookbook by Magnus Nilsson, who's the head chef at a top Swedish restaurant.

Get Back to Nature

Gain a more Nordic understanding by exploring nature.
https://pixabay.com/images/id-1072828/

If you have ever seen any documentaries or programs about the Nordic region, you can't have failed to notice the number of swimming pools, spas, and other outdoor leisure facilities. They don't see inclement weather as a reason to stay in and chill with Netflix. They see it as an opportunity to get out there and experience the joy of the great outdoors. Change your outlook and get in on Nordic by taking more adventurous holidays. No matter where you live, there will be an opportunity for you to take a break in nature. A cabin in the woods or a hiking holiday, it doesn't matter. Get rid of the luxuries and experience the joys of Mother Nature.

Take a Sauna

Cleansing should be both internal and external, and Nordic folk love to experience an intense sweat followed by an icy plunge into the water to create the juxtaposition between heat and cold. See if there is a traditional woodfired sauna near you to get those sweat glands working. There is nothing better after a stressful time than to relax in the steam, sweat out the toxins of life, and then immerse yourself in the freezing water.

To summarize, to celebrate trolldom and all things Nordic, you need to create a balance in your life, relationships, food, and emotions. However, you feel you can dip your toe by practicing cord magic and making cute bracelets, or you can go full-on Viking warrior. The choice is yours, and it always will be.

Bonus Section

A comprehensive guide to the potions from chapter 4 so you can print them and add them to your spell book or book of shadows.

The Hibiscus Love Potion

This simple herbal tea has no caffeine content and can be consumed both heated and cold. Make a batch to keep in the fridge for when you need a boost of self-confidence.

What You Need:

- Hibiscus tea
- Sugar
- Mint leaves
- Pink candle
- Small metal container
- Cup
- Water

Dress your altar with a candle and a white cloth. Turn off all your electronics and keep them out of your sacred area. Play soothing music or just enjoy the silence. Heat the water in the metal container with the candle flame while you recite the following "I am loved, I am worthy of that love, and I accept it with the power of the universe. Bring me a wave of inner peace, and let me rid myself of negativity and darkness while I let the light of the world fill me up."

Add the tea and water to your cup and sweeten to taste. Sprinkle the mint and drink after it has brewed. As you sip the tea, imagine your best life, that job you know you are worthy of, the partner you know you deserve, and see yourself surrounded by the love of people around you.

A Healing Potion for Low-Level Ailments or to Boost Energy

This is a simple brew that will make you feel energized and drive those nagging ailments away.

What You Need:

- 2 small pieces of willow bark
- 1 tbsp. vanilla extract
- 1 tbsp. apple juice
- A pinch of sage
- Pinch of rosemary
- 2 drops of lemon juice
- Water

Dress your altar with a light blue cloth and place the ingredients in your cauldron. Add your preferred base liquid; we have used water in this example and boiled the liquid. As the water boils, recite this mantra "Healing liquid be my balm, stop the pain and heal the harm." Once the liquid has cooled, pour it into a cup and sip the tea while imagining all the pain leaving your body. Imagine the white light filling you with energy and excitement for what the day holds for you, and picture the fatigue leaving your body and floating away into the ether.

Cold and Flu Potion

What You Need:

- Ginger, either dried or ground root
- 1 tbsp. lemon juice
- 1 tbsp. Manuka honey
- A pinch of cinnamon
- Brown sugar
- Water or lemon tea

This can be brewed on your altar or created in your kitchen on the stove. Add all the ingredients to a pot and let it simmer for ten minutes while you recite the following "Magic potion, do your thing, clear my throat so I can sing, let your magic soothe my soul and make me feel forever whole." Once the potion has cooled, sweeten it and drink whenever needed.

Protection Potion to Keep Negative Energy at Bay

This potion can be ingested to keep you safe or used to sprinkle around your home for added protection. It can be bottled and used for up to three months after it has been brewed.

What You Need:

- Jasmin tea bag
- 1 tbsp. Manuka honey
- 2 cloves
- 1 tbsp. lemon juice
- 3 bay leaves
- Sprinkle of black pepper
- Water
- Cup
- Sugar

Dress your altar in gold or red cloth and decorate with your favorite crystals or gemstones. Add anything you feel represents your favorite parts of your life, like your house keys, jewelry, or pictures of your family or friends.

Place the cauldron on the altar, add the ingredients (except the sugar), and repeat the following. "I call on the divine to make me feel safe. Bless me with your all-encompassing energy and shield me from harm. Be my guardian and give me the strength to shield others and myself."

Now take the cauldron to your kitchen and brew the potions. Use it to consecrate your home or drink it depending on your needs. Imagine a bright white dome surrounding all the things you love, and then picture the negative forces being repelled into the dark.

The Raspberry Honey Potion

This boozy potion is for cleansing and purifying your energy and attracting new love or friends

What You Need:

- Raspberry vodka
- Raspberry tea
- Hibiscus tea
- 1 tsp caramel syrup
- Lemon juice
- Honey
- Peppermint cordial
- Ice
- Cocktail shaker or cauldron

You can make the process more magical by dressing your altar in pink, yellow, or white cloths and a couple of candles, but this potion really is just about the end product. Add all the ingredients to your chosen receptacle and either stir or shake. Add the ice as you mix or put it in a glass to cool the liquid. As you sip your potion, thank the gods, goddesses, and the universe for your good fortune and give them cheers for their interest in you and your life.

Love Potion with Wine

What You Need:

- Wine, you can use white or rose
- Fresh peaches
- Raspberries
- Vanilla pods
- Sprig of mint
- Ice
- Glass

Fill a glass with ice and add the wine. As you add the other ingredients, ask the heavens to send you positive energy and a vision of your perfect partner. Once the potion has been stirred and chilled, sip it slowly and imagine how the two of you will look in the future. Thank the goddess of love and romance for her help.

Sleepy Potion

What You Need:
- 1 shot of dark rum
- Cinnamon
- Dark sugar
- Water or milk, depending on your taste
- An orange candle
- Lavender essence
- Cauldron
- Cup

Dress your altar with muted color cloth and place the orange candle on the surface. Put the rum, cinnamon, sugar, and water/milk in your cauldron on the stove and bring it to a boil before letting it simmer for two minutes. Bring the cauldron to the altar, light the candle, and sprinkle the essence on your altar as you pour the potion into a cup. Recite the following "Take me to the land of rest and let my sleep be the best, help me dream of past and present, and show me how to be ready for the future."

Drink the potion and let your eyes droop as you imagine the future filled with love and success.

Vino for Passion

What You Need:
- A bottle of sweet red or white wine
- 5 fresh basil leaves
- 6 red rose petals
- 3 cloves
- 4 apple seeds
- 2 drops of pomegranate essence

- 2 oz. raspberry juice
- A large piece of ginseng root
- Cauldron
- Tea cloth for straining
- Glass jar with a sealable top

Decorate your altar with red and white cloths, and then add white quartz, moonstone, and garnet to the table. Add all the ingredients to the cauldron and take it to the kitchen. Decorate the area you are working in with colored candles and tea lights. Stir the mixture over low heat and say, "I give this wine to show my love and hope they find it tasty, bring my love into my life and make their arrival hasty." As it cools, thank the goddess of love Freya for her ministrations and then bottle it. Keep it in the fridge until you find the person you feel is worthy of your love.

Money Comes to Me Potion

What You Need:
- 4 cups of water
- 2 sticks of cinnamon
- 4 cloves
- 1 tsp all spice powder
- 2 sprigs of fresh mint
- 2 tsp. brown sugar

Dress your altar in green and gold cloth and light a white candle anointed with your favorite oil. Place three-dollar bills on the altar. Take your cauldron to the kitchen and boil the water and all the other ingredients except the fresh mint for five minutes. Cover the cauldron and let the mixture steep for ten minutes off the heat. Repeat the following "Money and cash are nice to own. They make me happy and fill my soul if the universe wills it to bring that wealth and love to me."

Take the liquid and add the fresh mint. Leave it to cool before straining it and serving it with ice or as a reheated beverage. Feel the emotion you will experience as you receive your rewards while you sip the potion. After you have finished, thank the spirits for their help. For further strength, sprinkle the potion on the dollar bills and leave them on your altar.

Hocus Focus Potion

What You Need:

- 6 fresh lemons
- 4 cups of water
- A sprig of fresh rosemary
- Brown sugar
- Honey
- Lime juice
- Bay leaves
- Glass
- Ice

Make the basic juice by squeezing the lemons into three cups of water. As you squeeze, empower them by visualizing a smarter and sharper you after you have taken the potion. Imagine those awesome ideas you'll have and the positivity flowing from your mind. Set the juice aside to infuse with the rest of the ingredients.

On the stove, heat the remaining water with the rosemary, sugar, and honey. Let it boil for ten minutes until all the sugar has dissolved. Now let the mixture cool as you imagine the success you'll find in the future. That new job or the prospect of new experiences, let your senses become laser-focused on your future.

Add ice to a glass and pour in the lemon liquid. Remove the rosemary sprig and use the sweet liquid to enchant the lemony taste. Create a sweet elixir to promote your mental health and enjoy.

Bring the Heat Potion

What You Need:

- Sprig of rosemary
- ½ tsp thyme
- A pinch of sage
- A pinch of nutmeg
- 2 tsp mint tea leaves

- 3 cloves
- 3 rose petals
- 6 drops of lemon juice
- Water
- Picture of your loved one
- A piece of rose quartz

Set up your altar with red and pink cloths and light three white candles. Set the picture and the quartz in front of the middle white candles. Add the other ingredients to your cauldron and heat them over the candles, or take them into the kitchen and warm them on the stove.

As the mixture cools, repeat the following "Love and heat, fill me with hope and love. Let this tea bring the passion back to my love and me." Strain the liquid and sip it while you visualize the heat you two will bring to the bedroom.

Conclusion

Congratulations, you have traversed the frozen north and made it to the other side. So, are you now ready to live the life of the Nordic people? Is it the magic that appeals to you or the way of life? It is a personal choice, and however deep you become embroiled in Nordic ways, it's all good! Living a more virtuous life and getting back to basics can make you a better person; throw in some magical knowledge, and you are flying! Magic shouldn't just be something you wonder about, and it should be part of your regular life.

We would all benefit from some enchantment, mystery, and a touch of Nordic happiness, and trolldom is the perfect way to start. Give hygge living and the Scandi ways a try, and you are guaranteed to feel enlightened. Good luck on your journey, and remember to keep Nordic and embrace the trolls.

Here's another book by Mari Silva that you might like

Your Free Gift
(only available for a limited time)

Thanks for getting this book! If you want to learn more about various spirituality topics, then join Mari Silva's community and get a free guided meditation MP3 for awakening your third eye. This guided meditation mp3 is designed to open and strengthen ones third eye so you can experience a higher state of consciousness. Simply visit the link below the image to get started.

https://spiritualityspot.com/meditation

References

Futhark Magic: A Study of Ancient Runes - SnitchSeeker.com. (n.d.). Snitchseeker.Com. https://www.snitchseeker.com/term-27-january-april-2011/futhark-magic-a-study-of-ancient-runes-78018/

Dan. (2012, November 14). *Runes*. Norse Mythology for Smart People. https://norse-mythology.org/runes/

Dan. (2013, June 29). *Runic Philosophy and Magic*. Norse Mythology for Smart People. https://norse-mythology.org/runes/runic-philosophy-and-magic/

Gol stave church. (2019, April 13). Stavechurch.com. https://www.stavechurch.com/gol-stave-church/?lang=en

Harper, B. (2018, October 15). *47 Harry Potter spells to memorize while you're waiting for your Hogwarts letter*. Fatherly. https://www.fatherly.com/entertainment/25-harry-potter-spells-charms-everyone-should-know

McKay, A. (2020, August 21). *Viking runes: The historic writing systems of northern Europe*. Life in Norway. https://www.lifeinnorway.net/viking-runes/

Page, R. I. (1998). *Runes and runic inscriptions: Collected essays on Anglo-Saxon and viking runes*. Boydell Press.

Runemarks: Using runes. (n.d.). Joanne-harris.co.uk. http://www.joanne-harris.co.uk/books/runemarks/runemarks-using-runes/

Runer og magi. (n.d.). Avaldsnes. https://avaldsnes.info/en/viking/lorem-ipsum/

S., J. (2021, April 27). *How to read rune stones*. Norse and Viking Mythology [Best Blog] - Vkngjewelry; vkngjewelry. https://blog.vkngjewelry.com/en/rune-divination-how-to-read-the-runes/

Sørensen, A. C., & Horte, R. M. J. (n.d.). *Runes*. Vikingeskibsmuseet i Roskilde. https://www.vikingeskibsmuseet.dk/en/professions/education/viking-age-people/runes

Thornton, A. (2022, June 11). *Norse runes: Ultimate guide to the Vikings' Nordic alphabet*. Seek Scandinavia; Houseplant Authority. https://seekscandinavia.com/norse-runes/

Viking runes and runestones. (2014, June 8). History. https://www.historyonthenet.com/viking-runes-and-runestones

Wigington, P. (2008, December 22). *The Norse Runes - A basic overview*. Learn Religions. https://www.learnreligions.com/norse-runes-basic-overview-2562815

Williams, J. A. (n.d.). *The power and mystery of the runes*. Curious Historian https://curioushistorian.com/the-power-and-mystery-of-the-runes

Zhelyazkov, Y. (2022, February 2). *Norse runes explained – meaning and symbolism*. Symbol Sage. https://symbolsage.com/norse-runes-meaning-symbolism/

(N.d.-a). Holisticshop.co.uk. https://www.holisticshop.co.uk/articles/guide-runes

(N.d.-b). Viking-styles.com https://viking-styles.com/blogs/history/runes

20 Children of Odin: Who are they? (2021, May 15). Myth Nerd. https://mythnerd.com/children-of-odin/

Balder – loved by everyone. (n.d.). Historiska.Se. https://historiska.se/norse-mythology/balder-en/

Dan. (2012a, November 14). *Norse mythology for Smart People - the ultimate online guide to Norse mythology and religion*. Norse Mythology for Smart People. https://norse-mythology.org/

Dan. (2012b, November 15). *Bifrost*. Norse Mythology for Smart People. https://norse-mythology.org/cosmology/bifrost/

Dan. (2012c, November 15). *Fenrir*. Norse Mythology for Smart People. https://norse-mythology.org/gods-and-creatures/giants/fenrir/

Dan. (2012d, November 15). *Freyr*. Norse Mythology for Smart People. https://norse-mythology.org/gods-and-creatures/the-vanir-gods-and-goddesses/freyr/

Dan. (2012e, November 15). *Jormungand*. Norse Mythology for Smart People. https://norse-mythology.org/gods-and-creatures/giants/jormungand/

Dan. (2012f, November 15). *Muspelheim*. Norse Mythology for Smart People. https://norse-mythology.org/cosmology/the-nine-worlds/muspelheim/

Dan. (2012g, November 15). *Odin's Discovery of the runes*. Norse Mythology for Smart People. https://norse-mythology.org/tales/odins-discovery-of-the-runes/

Dan. (2012h, November 15). *Ragnarok*. Norse Mythology for Smart People. https://norse-mythology.org/tales/ragnarok/

Dan. (2012i, November 15). *The Creation of Thor's Hammer.* Norse Mythology for Smart People. https://norse-mythology.org/tales/loki-and-the-dwarves/

Dan. (2012j, November 15). *The Death of Baldur.* Norse Mythology for Smart People. https://norse-mythology.org/tales/the-death-of-baldur/

Dan. (2012k, November 15). *The Norns.* Norse Mythology for Smart People. https://norse-mythology.org/gods-and-creatures/others/the-norns/

Dan. (2012l, November 15). *Valhalla.* Norse Mythology for Smart People. https://norse-mythology.org/cosmology/valhalla/

Dan. (2012m, November 15). *Why Odin is one-Eyed.* Norse Mythology for Smart People. https://norse-mythology.org/tales/why-odin-is-one-eyed/

Dan. (2012n, November 15). *Yggdrasil.* Norse Mythology for Smart People. https://norse-mythology.org/cosmology/yggdrasil-and-the-well-of-urd/

Dan. (2014, May 20). *Skoll and Hati.* Norse Mythology for Smart People. https://norse-mythology.org/skoll-hati/

Elly, M. (2018a, May 11). *The punishment of Loki.* BaviPower. https://bavipower.com/blogs/bavipower-viking-blog/the-punishment-of-loki

Elly, M. (2018b, July 6). *Odin's Sons in Norse Myth.* BaviPower. https://bavipower.com/blogs/bavipower-viking-blog/odins-sons-in-norse-myth

Manea, I.-M. (2022). Magic rings in Norse mythology. *World History Encyclopedia.* https://www.worldhistory.org/article/1950/magic-rings-in-norse-mythology/

Mark, J. J. (2021). Sif. *World History Encyclopedia.* https://www.worldhistory.org/Sif/

No title. (n.d.). Study.com. https://study.com/academy/lesson/what-is-norse-mythology-overview-deities-stories.html

Damian, Angel. "TROLLS! Discover 7 Strange Facts about These Mythical Creatures." Themagichoroscope.com, 29 Jan. 2020, https://themagichoroscope.com/zodiac/mythical-creatures-trolls

"Get to Know the Magic of the Celtic Tree Calendar." Learn Religions, www.learnreligions.com/celtic-tree-months-2562403

"Home." The Trolldom Society, www.thetrolldomsociety.org/.

https://www.facebook.com/bohdi.sanders . "Bodhi Sanders." The Wisdom Warrior, 31 Mar. 2018, https://thewisdomwarrior.com/2010/09/17/the-nine-noble-virtues-viking-values-for-the-warrior-lifestyle/

"My 10 Best Witchcraft Tips for Beginners." Orion the Witch, 7 Aug. 2019, www.orionthewitch.com/10-tips-beginner-witchcraft/#:~:text=My%2010%20Best%20Witchcraft%20Tips%20for%20Beginners%201

"Online Spell Book." Free Witchcraft Spells

Seal, Graham. "THE BLACK BOOK – Dealing with Demons." GRISTLY HISTORY, 1 Dec. 2020, https://gristlyhistory.blog/2020/12/01/the-black-book-dealing-with-demons/

Studios, Clockpunk. "Dwarf Magic." Altearth, www.altearth.net/articles/history-nations/dwarves/dwarf-magic/

team, The Stylist web. "How to Live Nordicly: Achieving Health and Happiness with Tips from the Frozen North." Stylist, 13 June 2016, www.stylist.co.uk/life/how-to-live-nordicly-scandinavia-sweden-norway-denmark-iceland-health-happiness-tips/64781

"The Key of Hell." Astonishing Legends, www.astonishinglegends.com/astonishing-legends/2019/5/11/the-key-of-hell

"The Ultimate Guide to Magical Herbs for Spells & Rituals - TheMagickalCat.com." Www.themagickalcat.com, 18 Nov. 2020, www.themagickalcat.com/magical-herbs-guide

"Using Magical Crystals & Gemstones." Learn Religions, www.learnreligions.com/magical-crystals-and-gemstones-2562758#:~:text=%20Magical%20Crystals%20and%20Gemstones%20%201%20Agate..

"What Are Trolls? Exploring the Mystery of Scandinavian Trolls." Scandification, 30 Jan. 2020, https://scandification.com/exploring-the-mystery-of-scandinavian-trolls/

WiseWitch. "Powerful Cord and Knot Magick." Wise Witches and Witchcraft

Yong, Ced. "The Epic List of 250 Legendary Swords from Mythology, Folklore, and Fiction." HobbyLark, https://hobbylark.com/fandoms/The-Epic-List-of-250-Legendary-Swords#:~:text=Mistilteinn%3A%20In%20Norse%20mythology%2C%20the%20magical%20sword%20of

Seal, Graham. "THE BLACK BOOK – Dealing with Demons." GRISTLY HISTORY, 1 Dec. 2020, https://gristlyhistory.blog/2020/12/01/the-black-book-dealing-with-demons/

Studios, Clockpunk. "Dwarf Magic." Altearth, www.altearth.net/articles/history-nations/dwarves/dwarf-magic/

team, The Stylist web. "How to Live Nordicly: Achieving Health and Happiness with Tips from the Frozen North." Stylist, 13 June 2016, www.stylist.co.uk/life/how-to-live-nordicly-scandinavia-sweden-norway-denmark-iceland-health-happiness-tips/64781

"The Key of Hell." Astonishing Legends, www.astonishinglegends.com/astonishing-legends/2019/5/11/the-key-of-hell

"The Ultimate Guide to Magical Herbs for Spells & Rituals - TheMagickalCat.com." Www.themagickalcat.com, 18 Nov. 2020, www.themagickalcat.com/magical-herbs-guide

"Using Magical Crystals & Gemstones." Learn Religions, www.learnreligions.com/magical-crystals-and-gemstones-2562758#:~:text=%20Magical%20Crystals%20and%20Gemstones%20%201%20Agate..

"What Are Trolls? Exploring the Mystery of Scandinavian Trolls." Scandification, 30 Jan. 2020, https://scandification.com/exploring-the-mystery-of-scandinavian-trolls/

WiseWitch. "Powerful Cord and Knot Magick." Wise Witches and Witchcraft

Yong, Ced. "The Epic List of 250 Legendary Swords from Mythology, Folklore, and Fiction." HobbyLark, https://hobbylark.com/fandoms/The-Epic-List-of-250-Legendary-Swords#:~:text=Mistilteinn%3A%20In%20Norse%20mythology%2C%20the%20magical%20sword%20of